Interpersonal Relationships

With a more specific focus than the all-encompassing textbook, each title in the Foundations of Psychology series enables students who are new to psychology to get to grips with a key area of psychological research, while also developing an understanding of basic concepts, debates and research methodologies. In this book Diana Jackson-Dwyer presents an introductory survey of classic and recent research on relationships and the theories that underpin them.

Topics covered include:

- the place of relationships within the history of psychology
- the evolutionary roots of relationships
- research methodologies
- different kinds of relationship: kinship, friendship, loving and mating.

There are also discussions of a range of issues, informed by recent research: from rising divorce rates to cultural variations in mating patterns, the issue of gay marriage and the effect of the internet on relationships.

Each chapter contains numerous pedagogical features which will help students to engage with the material, including:

- chapter-specific learning objectives and summaries of key points
- study boxes presenting reflective exercises, research questions and issues for discussion
- glossaries and suggestions for further reading.

Assuming no prior knowledge of the subject, *Interpersonal Relationships* provides an accessible and up-to-date overview of this vibrant area of psychology. The book will be ideal reading for those who are new to higher-level study – whether they are at school or college, or first-year undergraduate students taking introductory courses in psychology.

Diana Jackson-Dwyer taught in Further Education for 20 years, during which time she was Head of Psychology organising a large team of lecturers and teaching psychology on a variety of courses. She is also an experienced examiner at GCSE and A-level, and has written psychology books for GCSE and criminal psychology courses, as well as A-level revision guides.

Foundations of Psychology Series

This series provides pre-undergraduate and first year undergraduates with appealing and useful books that will enable the student to expand their knowledge of key areas in psychology. The books go beyond the detail and discussion provided by general introductory books but will still be accessible and appropriate for this level. This series will bridge the gap between the all-encompassing general textbook and the currently available advanced topic-specific books which might be inaccessible to students who are studying such topics for the first time. Each book has a contemporary focus and fits into one of three main categories including Themes and Perspectives (such as Theoretical Approaches or Ethics), Specific Topics (such as Memory or Relationships) and Applied Areas (such as Psychology and Crime).

Series Editors

Philip Banyard is a Reader in Psychology at Nottingham Trent University.

Cara Flanagan is an experienced academic author, writer and freelance lecturer in Psychology.

Published Titles

Cultural Issues in Psychology
Andrew Stevenson

Ethical Issues in Psychology
Philip Banyard and Cara Flanagan

Essentials of Sensation and Perception
George Mather

Interpersonal Relationships
Diana Jackson-Dwyer

Interpersonal Relationships

Diana Jackson-Dwyer

Routledge
Taylor & Francis Group

LONDON AND NEW YORK

First published 2014
by Routledge
27 Church Road, Hove, East Sussex BN3 2FA

and by Routledge
711 Third Avenue, New York, NY 10017

Routledge is an imprint of the Taylor & Francis Group, an informa business

British Library Cataloguing in Publication Data
A catalogue record for this book is available from the British Library

Library of Congress Cataloging in Publication Data
Jackson-Dwyer, Diana, 1949–
    Interpersonal relationships / Diana Jackson-Dwyer.
    pages cm.—(Foundations of psychology)
    Includes bibliographical references and index.
    1. Interpersonal relations. I. Title.
    HM1106.J33 2013
    302—dc23
    2013008752

ISBN: 978–0–415–42915–3 (hbk)
ISBN: 978–0–415–42916–0 (pbk)
ISBN: 978–0–203–79785–3 (ebk)

Typeset in Arial and Frutiger
by Swales & Willis Ltd, Exeter, Devon

MIX
Paper from
responsible sources
FSC   FSC® C013056
www.fsc.org

Printed and bound in Great Britain by
TJ International Ltd, Padstow, Cornwall

This book is dedicated to two very special people with whom it has been my great privilege to have a mutually loving relationship.

To my sister Penny Rundle, who, despite her name, is priceless; an invaluable friend through thick and thin (and such fun).

To my husband Len Jackson, light of my life, who has given me happiness beyond my imagining. It's never too late to make wonderful relationships!

My thanks to Sam Jackson and Andrew Whitfield for allowing me to use photos of their daughter Ellie, our beautiful granddaughter.

Contents

List of illustrations

Figures

Tables

In the beginning

The roots of relationships

1

What this chapter will teach you

- The context of the study of relationships within psychology.

- Why attachments are important to our survival.

- The ways in which a baby is innately pre-programmed to develop attachments.

- What is meant by affiliation and how it affects us.

No man is an island, entire of itself.
—John Donne.

Humans are essentially social beings. As countless novels, films, songs, plays and poems testify, our ultimate happiness and despair is founded in **relationships**. Satisfaction at work, at play and in family life depends largely on the quality of our friendships and loves. When Klinger (1977) posed the question 'What is it that makes your life meaningful?', almost all respondents (89%) mentioned one or another kind of personal relationship as something that contributed

> **KEY TERM**
>
> **Relationship** A relationship exists to the extent that two people exert strong, frequent and diverse effects on one another over an extended period of time.

meaning to their lives; for many it was the only thing they mentioned. Friendship is of paramount importance to most of us: in one survey it was rated over power, recognition, excitement and a comfortable life by 85% of people (Bibby 2001).

Relationships contribute both to our most uplifting experiences and to our darkest. On the positive side they are a source of life satisfaction and well-being; they contribute to good mental and physical health as well as longevity. On the negative side, poor relationships can cause enormous stress and the lack of them is a source of loneliness and isolation. In essence, although relationships can be hell, we can't live without them. 'They are an unlimited, indefinitely sustainable resource that we can all enjoy and from which we can all benefit' (Perlman 2007, p. 14).

So what is a relationship? There is such a huge variety of relationships – those with lovers, family, teammates, co-workers, neighbours, the local shopkeeper, your doctor – that this is not a simple question to answer, although we all probably know one when we see it. A useful definition is offered by Kelley *et al.* (1983) who suggest that *a relationship exists to the extent that two people exert strong, frequent and diverse effects on one another over an extended period of time.* Whatever the definition, most relationships include the following three aspects: interdependence, need fulfilment and emotional attachment.

It's important to remember that although we may think of relationships as based on emotions and feelings, in fact they are things we *do.* They occur in the context of everyday life; in fact they *are* everyday life: shopping, gossiping, working, sorting out our leisure activities, discussing the news, deciding what to have for dinner (Duck 2007).

The study of relationships within psychology

Given their huge importance in our lives, it is hardly surprising that relationships have been a major preoccupation of philosophers and writers since recorded history began. Within psychology they crop up in many areas due to the fact that they influence so much of our behaviour that there are interpersonal aspects in most branches of the discipline. Some of the most important are:

- Freud's theory: the role of parent–child relationships in personality development.
- Developmental psychology: how personality is shaped by a person's attachment history.
- Social psychology: how people influence and are influenced by others, e.g. social facilitation; social loafing; conformity and obedience.

- Personality theories including the Big Five theory, in which two of these facets, extroversion and agreeableness have obvious interpersonal ramifications.
- Cognitive psychology: how babies are 'prewired' to have cognitive abilities that facilitate the formation of relationships, e.g. the ability to visually track a human face virtually from birth; language acquisition.
- Health psychology: the recognition that any comprehensive intervention involving both physical and mental health must take account of people's relationships.

Given this, it is perhaps surprising that interpersonal relationships was not a dedicated topic area in psychology with an empirical body of knowledge until the 1980s. It's true that there were precursors to this: there was research in the 1960s and 70s but it concentrated mainly on studies of attraction with the result that a huge amount of information was gathered about one rather narrow field. We learnt about the influence of good looks, that similar people rather than opposites attract, and that proximity has a great influence on attraction. Research methods were limited, mainly laboratory studies in which samples of college students were asked for their almost immediate reactions to strangers, or responses to a bogus person who had completed an attitude questionnaire. In the latter case, absolutely no contact between real-life people ever took place. Duck (1995) complained that such research did not look at many of the run-of-the-mill interactions involved in everyday life, such as playfulness and joking, managing routines like cooking, cleaning and bathing the children, and the mutual understanding that derives from such ordinary interchange.

Recognising these limitations, and probably in recognition of rising divorce rates, the 1980s onwards saw an upsurge in the study of established relationships: what makes them stable or unstable, happy or unhappy, enduring or short-lived? Researchers began to investigate the link between relationships and many areas of well-being, including life satisfaction, longevity, the treatment of many forms of mental illness, the strength of the immune system and effectiveness both at work and school. Research into interpersonal relationships became far broader and now presents a much more complex picture of human relationships. It includes not only the positive elements – the delights, laughter and joy of friendship, romance and family – but also the negative elements – the irritations and annoyances that we all recognise as part and parcel of relationships. It also tends to look at the course of real-life relationships over a considerable period of time and thereby investigates the factors that contribute to satisfaction, dissatisfaction and the means by which we deal with the changes in our feelings towards other people. In addition, research has looked at the profound effect relationships have on our health, both physical and mental. Such research has a wide variety of practical applications and contributes greatly to our understanding of what makes us happy and fulfilled and what makes us profoundly miserable.

This research, however, is tough! Just as no person is an island, so no relationship is an island – they all exist within a social context. Think of any relationship in which you are involved (workmates, friends, marriage partner, family) and you will see immediately that all them are part of a complex network of other relationships, not simply an emotional experience between two people. This factor, combined with the enormous variety of relationship types, provides a great challenge to researchers in relationships.

Theoretical perspectives

There is no single theory that unifies relationship research but it is helpful to outline some of the major theoretical perspectives that have emerged within this field. They are not mutually exclusive, rather the reverse since attachment theory is based on evolutionary theory.

Reinforcement theories

These were very influential in the early research and are still important today. **Reinforcement theories** are based on the premise that people behave in a way that is rewarding to them. They initiate and remain in relationships that have positive outcomes but once the balance is tipped towards the negative then these relationships are unlikely to survive. This is the basis of a variety of theories including social exchange theory, interdependence theory and equity theory, as discussed in Chapter 4.

Evolutionary psychology

This is a later entrant to the stage but of enormous influence in this field. **Evolutionary psychology** is guided by the principle that behaviour is influenced by evolved biological mechanisms. This perspective argues that humans are social animals because group living enhances their chances of survival and reproduction. In consequence, humans have evolved the need to form relationships.

KEY TERMS

Reinforcement theories Theories based on the assumption that people behave in ways which are rewarding to them and desist from behaviour that has adverse consequences.

Evolutionary psychology This approach looks at the way in which behaviour has been influenced by evolved biological mechanisms that enhances survival and/or survival of offspring.

Attachment theory This theory states that the first relationship a child has with its caregiver profoundly affects later relationships, especially in terms of what a person comes to expect in terms of support and trustworthiness.

Attachment theory

This emphasises not only our evolved biological tendencies but also the influence that our early experience of relationships has on our capacity to engage in satisfying relationships later in life. According to **attachment theory**, the caregiver–infant relationship profoundly affects what a child comes to expect in terms of support, empathy and trustworthiness.

Affiliation, attachment and the need for social contact

Humans possess no impressive physical abilities: we have no sharp teeth or claws, no outstanding visual capabilities; we can't run fast or leap from tree to tree. We have no warm coat and, in most climates, could not survive without artificial help. Our children are born utterly helpless and remain incapable of independent existence for many years. Given these limitations, how have we climbed to the top of the evolutionary ladder?

The challenge in human evolution is the same for all species – reproduction and development of offspring to reproductive age. If we have not risen to this challenge via physical capabilities, the key to our success may lie in human sociality (Caporeal 2007). Many of the abilities that enable humans to adapt to a wide variety of physical environment are dependent on cooperation and collective knowledge both within and between generations. Social groups defend people against environmental hazards, predators and hostile outsiders. Social groups enable tasks to be shared so that those who are protecting the vulnerable young can be provided for by others who hunt and forage for food. Information, as well as tasks, can be shared so that actions can be coordinated to the advantage of the whole group. Most tasks are more easily completed successfully when people do them together rather than alone, whether grinding grain, harvesting fruit or hunting large animals. Evolutionary pressures, therefore, have led us to live in close proximity to other people for purposes of protection and to form groups that help solve the problems involved in survival and reproduction more effectively. Natural selection has, to this end, produced a strong motive for **affiliation** as part of the human psyche.

> **KEY TERM**
>
> **Affiliation** Seeking the company of others and interacting with them in a positive manner.

The need to belong

Baumeister and Leary (1995) have argued that humans have evolved a need to belong, which is a fundamental motivation.

The **belongingness hypothesis** states that humans need to 'form and maintain strong, stable interpersonal relationships' and that this need 'is a powerful, fundamental, and extremely pervasive motivation' (p. 497). According to these researchers, we therefore have an innate need both to affiliate – that is, to seek the company of others – and to form and maintain a number of positive, lasting and significant interpersonal relationships. This need can only be satisfied by frequent interaction with familiar people combined with persistent caring. Since this need can be almost as compelling as a need for food, human culture is shaped by the necessity to provide belongingness.

The belongingness hypothesis is consistent with the following characteristics of humans (Baumeister & Leary 1995).

- People in all cultures form into groups; social bonds form very easily within any society.
- Babies have an innate need to form attachments and form them with their caregivers very early in life (Bowlby 1969 – see later in this chapter). Throughout life, people form attachments readily and eagerly and resist breaking them.
- A great deal of human cognitive processing is devoted to abilities such as language and empathy with facilitate interpersonal relationships.
- Many psychological studies, as well as everyday observations, demonstrate that humans form into groups and show group allegiance even when there are no obvious benefits (e.g. Sherif *et al.* 1961; Tajfel 1970)
- Many of the strongest emotions people experience are concerned with human relationships. People greatly enjoy belonging and being needed but have a fear and dislike of being rejected. People experience happiness, elation and contentment when relationships are going well, and anxiety, depression, grief, jealousy and loneliness when they are not.
- People are adversely affected by lack of attachment in terms of well-being, adjustment and health. People who lack belongingness have high levels of mental and physical illness (e.g. Berkman *et al.* 2000; Williams *et al.* 2000).

The need to attach

Many developmental psychologists suggest that, because of the need of humans to form relationships in order to survive, the first specific relationship that an infant makes is very important in their later development. This relationship is referred to as an **attachment**, which can be defined as *a long-enduring, emotionally meaningful tie to a particular individual* (Schaffer 1996). Foremost of these psychologists who theorise on attachment is Bowlby (1969, 1988) who put forward a theory of attachment that be summarised as follows:

> **KEY TERM**
>
> **Attachment** A long-lasting, emotionally meaningful tie to a particular individual.

1 Children have a biological need to attach to one person and they are 'pre-programmed' to make such an attachment. From birth the human baby possesses a number of inborn behaviour patterns, such as clinging, smiling and crying which serve to bind the child to the caregiver right from the start.

2 The main attachment process begins around 7 months just before the baby can crawl, so that he or she is unlikely to move too far away from the main caregiver and therefore remains safe.

3 The bond that a child develops with its main caregiver (often the mother) is a very special one, different from other bonds that a child develops. Bowlby referred to this tendency to bond to one main person as **monotropy**.

> **KEY TERM**
>
> **Monotropy** An innate tendency to form an attachment to one specific individual. This type of attachment is different from all others and much stronger.

4 There is a critical period from about 7 months to 3 years, during which the baby is most likely to form this attachment bond and that if it is not formed then, it is unlikely to form at all, and the child will probably not form a permanent attachment to anyone.

5 Since the first attachment serves as an internal working model, which is the basis of our expectations and rules regarding relationships in later life, the consequences of not forming this crucial bond are liable to be very damaging.

Some aspects of Bowlby's theory have been very controversial. For example, Schaffer and Emerson (1964) demonstrated that attachment does not appear to be monotropic. These researchers contend that children often form multiple attachments with no single attachment being more important than others. Nevertheless, despite specific criticism, there seems little doubt that attachments are crucial in a young child's life and that the nature of these attachments have long-term consequences.

The stages of attachment

There are several phases or stages in the development of attachment (Schaffer & Emerson 1964). First of all, children are *universally sociable*: by 6 weeks they smile at anyone and do not care who responds to them. Once they are able to discriminate among individuals they begin to show marked preferences which become more marked over the following few months. From the second and third months children seem capable of recognising particular faces and thereafter are more likely to smile in response to familiar people, such as members of the family. Less familiar individuals will elicit only weak smiles. A milestone in attachment occurs around 7 months when the first strong attachment appears. At about the same time, infants exhibit 'stranger anxiety', that is, they become wary of unfamiliar people. Once babies are mobile, attachment behaviour includes moving towards, staying close, separation protest, clinging and using the adult as a 'secure base' from which to explore. Very soon after the first main attachment has been formed, the infant starts to form additional attachments with others who he or she sees consistently and with whom they have a mutually enjoyable time. This will typically include father, grandparent, older sibling, perhaps a close friend of the family. Margaret Mead (1962) argued that the tendency to form multiple attachments is biologically useful since it reduces the amount of distress caused to the infant if the main caregiver (usually the mother) should die when the child is still very young, a common occurrence in all cultures at one time and still today in many.

Individual variations in attachment

Ainsworth and her colleagues (e.g. Ainsworth *et al.* 1978) have investigated in detail the nature of the attachment bond. She devised a structured observation study known as the Strange Situation in order to investigate the relationship between the caregiver and young child. In a Strange Situation study, the child and mother (or caregiver) are put into an unfamiliar room containing interesting toys and observed through a one-way mirror. After a short while a stranger enters and soon after that the mother leaves. The mother then returns and the stranger leaves. The mother then leaves again, so the child is now alone. The mother then returns. At all stages the child's reactions are observed with particular interest taken in four types of behaviour. First, the response the child makes when the mother departs (known as separation anxiety). Second, the infants' willingness to explore and play with the new toys. Third, the reaction of the child to the stranger (called stranger anxiety). Fourth, reunion behaviour, that is, how the child behaves when the mother returns.

Table 1.1 The Strange Situation procedure

Episode	What happens
1	The mother (or caregiver) takes the infant into the laboratory room and sits quietly in a chair. She does not interact with the infant unless the child tries to attract her attention.
2	A stranger enters, talks to the mother and then approaches the baby with a toy.
3	The mother leaves quietly without drawing attention to herself. If the infant does seem bothered, the stranger tries to interact by talking to him or her and playing. If the child shows distress, the stranger attempts to comfort him or her.
4	The mother returns and greets the infant. The stranger leaves. The mother tries to get the infant to play, then leaves, waving and saying "bye-bye".
5	The baby is left alone.
6	The stranger enters and interacts with the infant, offering comfort if the child is upset or a toy if the child is passive.
7	The mother returns, greets the infant and picks him/her up. The stranger leaves quietly.

Source: From Dwyer and Roberts (2009). Psychology for GCSE level (2nd edn, p. 168).

From these studies Ainsworth concluded that infants have very different types of attachment to their caregiver and she classified these types of attachment as follows:

Secure attachment (Type B): infants explore freely when their mother is present and use her as a secure base when the stranger appears. They show distress when she leaves and greet her warmly when she returns. They are readily comforted by her, soon returning to a state of contentment, and show a clear preference for her over the stranger. This is the optimum form of attachment.

Resistant (anxious) attachment (Type C): children do not explore the new toys with such confidence. Compared to secure infants, they remain closer to their mother, showing signs of insecurity even in her presence. They become very distressed when she leaves. When she returns they may cling to her but show ambivalent reactions such as hitting her while still clinging. They are clearly angry and anxious. She does not provide a secure base.

Avoidant attachment (Type A): children show little or no concern when the mother leaves or pleasure when she returns. There is no indication of stranger anxiety and the children show little preference for the mother over the stranger, often avoiding both.

Later, a fourth type of attachment was added (Main & Solomon 1986).

Disorganised, insecure attachment (Type D): children show no set pattern of behaviour when the mother departs or when she returns (hence 'disorganised'). This kind of behaviour is associated with abused children or those whose mothers are chronically depressed.

Although, as you can see, there is a variety of attachment types, the most important distinction is that of secure (Type B) as opposed to insecure (Types A,C,D) attachment.

Long term effects of attachment

As we have seen, Bowlby believed that all babies have a biological need for a warm, intimate and continuous relationship with the mother or substitute mother. This need, according to Bowlby, is as basic as the need for food, warmth and so on. Children who do not have this need satisfactorily met may suffer from what he termed *maternal deprivation*, which was said to occur when a child under the age of three is deprived of his or her mother for a period of at least three months, or has a number of changes of mother figure.

Bowlby, supported by others including Ainsworth, believes that the type of attachment a child first forms acts as an *internal working model for all later social relationships* and helps to shape all intimate interpersonal relationships in later life. Put in very basic terms, this means that those children who are subject to very insecure attachments in early life are liable to be untrusting and insecure in all later relationships, including friendships, romantic relationships and those with their own children. Hazan and Shaver (1987) argue that the type of attachment experienced in infancy shapes all types of relationships, especially romantic ones, in later life. Their work is discussed in Chapter 5.

Bowlby, who worked extensively with adolescents with serious emotional and behavioural problems, believed that in some of the most severe cases of deprivation, a child may, as an adult, be unable to make relationships with other people or have any real feelings of empathy or sympathy for anyone, a so-called **affectionless personality**. Such children or adults are often superficially sociable but have no real concern for others or capacity to care for people. They fail to develop a conscience or feelings of guilt, and tend to be persistent liars, thieves or psychopaths. This inability to form deep bonds applies to the way they feel about their own children, so their own infants may find bonding difficult or impossible.

KEY TERM

Affectionless personality An inability show affection or concern for others or to form long-term meaningful relationships.

REFLECTIVE EXERCISE 1.1

Bowlby's theories have been the subject of much criticism over the years. Some of this may be deserved but a lot of it is based on ignorance of his original work. As a student you must be careful to refer to the original source on occasion in order to judge the fairness of any evaluation.

One example is that Bowlby is cited as saying that the effects of early deprivation or privation are inevitable and irreversible. He said no such thing. What he did say was that an affectionless character does not develop easily. According to him, because all children are biologically biased to form an attachment to the person looking after them, they will do so even if abused. It is only rarely, after repeated experiences of separation, that children become permanently emotionally detached and 'affectionless'. In addition, Bowlby never disputed the fact that some children who are the victims of deprivation in their early lives do escape delinquency and other damage. He estimated that only around 25 per cent of them are likely to suffer irreparable damage. However, because this damage is so considerable, we should do all we can to avoid it. He made a comparison with polio vaccination – although only around 1% of children who get polio are damaged by it, we still protect against it; so we should take every precaution to protect our children against the possible damage done if their attachments are broken.

Try to make time to read some of Bowlby's original work.

Baby's adaptiveness: the caregiving system

Consistent with the argument that the need to belong is innate and has been programmed by natural selection, human infants, helpless though they may be, are born with a rich biological inheritance that enables them to form social relationships with familiar people and to differentiate familiar people from strangers. The following are some of these abilities.

Face recognition

Virtually from birth human babies have a particular interest in human faces (Mondloch *et al.* 1999) and will stare intently at them. By measuring the extent to which infants follow various moving stimuli with their eyes and turn their heads, Morton and Johnson (1991) found significantly greater responses to face-like than to non-face-like stimuli for infants ranging from several minutes to 5 weeks old. This suggests that infants are born with some idea of 'faceness'. The pioneer of this research, Robert Fantz, wrote that this preference for face-like patterns may 'play an important role in the development of behaviour by focusing attention to stimuli that later have adaptive significance' (Fantz 1961, p. 72).

Faces provide the richest and most reliable clues to feelings and behavioural intentions (Hassin & Trope 2000). Cognitive neuroscientists have suggested that humans have evolved a specialised face-processing module in the brain (Farah 2000) and they have tentatively concluded that such a module is independent of recognition of objects (Gazzaniga *et al.* 1998).

Differentiation between faces

It is essential for babies to be able to differentiate between familiar people and strangers. As they become exposed to more and more faces in their everyday lives babies focus on the kinds of faces they see most often and tune out other types (Pascalis *et al.* 2002).

Empathic accuracy

One fascinating feature of humans is the ability to perceive and understand another's emotions. This begins, albeit it in a fairly unsophisticated way, very early: by 4 months of age infants smile more at smiling

Figure 1.1 Even though she is only 24 hours old, Ellie stares intently at the face of her granddad.

than at non-smiling faces (Oster *et al.* 1989). As they get older, the degree of empathy they show increases and they can easily interpret a tone of voice, a raised eyebrow and the emotions shown by a frown, a smile or a sad expression. The importance of empathetic understanding of others' emotions and thoughts in interaction can be appreciated when we study autistic children lacking this ability who are therefore prone to many misunderstandings in social interaction. Buck and Ginsberg (1997) believe that empathy involves 'a biologically based, spontaneous communication process that is fundamental to all living things'. This ability allows people to coordinate their activities for their mutual benefit and facilitates bonding with others.

Communication

From birth babies appear both ready and motivated to communicate and share meaning with others. By 2 months of age infants engage in complex, highly responsive interactions with their main caregivers. These communications involve give-and-take exchanges in the form of coos, gazes, smiles, grunts and sucks! During the first 6 months infants develop a growing awareness of the characteristics of those people who are part of their social world. These early interactions lay the foundation for the understanding of self and others.

Language

Language is a fundamental tool of communication and babies appear to be well prepared for its acquisition. The pioneering linguist Noam Chomsky (1957) proposed that children are born with a 'mental organ' specially designed for the acquisition of language. Infants also have impressive prelinguistic skills: as early as the first days of life, newborn babies regulate their behaviour to synchronise with the pattern of human speech, showing small but consistent bodily movements in response to the rhythmic sounds of normal speech (e.g. Condon & Sandor 1974). In this way babies participate in rudimentary social interaction. Speech in any language evokes these synchronised body movements but environmental sounds or nonsense speech do not. It seems that, from birth, newborns are particularly responsive to the regular patterns of meaningful speech and, in their own way, can differentiate between random noise or vocalisations and genuine social signals.

Characteristics that elicit caregiving behaviour

Infants do not only possess specific innate behavioural patterns that encourage relationship formation, they also possess certain

Figure 1.2 Ellie's reaction to mum demonstrates how babies are innately prewired to be receptive to making relationships.

characteristics that elicit caregiving behaviour in adults. Ethologists such as Lorenz and Bowlby believe that caregiving behaviour is triggered by infants' immature features (large eyes, round cheeks, flat nose and short limbs). Another vital communication and survival tool possessed by infants is their crying behaviour. As many of us have observed to our considerable discomfort and distress, infant cries are powerful stimuli to elicit adult attention and are extremely difficult to ignore.

Affiliation

Fundamental to the formation of any relationships is the tendency to affiliate – that is, to associate or interact with other people. As we have already discussed, natural selection has probably forged a strong motive for affiliation as part of the human psyche.

Motives for affiliation

Hill (1987) suggests that are four main motives for affiliation:

- to obtain positive stimulation
- to obtain emotional support
- to gain social comparison information
- to get attention from other people.

To obtain positive stimulation

People inherently enjoy the company of others (again, probably for evolutionary reasons already discussed), so mixing with friends and, even sometimes strangers, provides a positive experience. Brain imaging studies (e.g. Harris *et al.* 2007) indicate that the same regions of the brain are activated by simply interacting with other people as by other social rewards, indicating that people like to associate with other people simply for its own sake. Naturally, the desire to affiliate is affected by the particular people with whom we are interacting or the specific situation: the desire to affiliate increases if the people and/or situation are interesting and fun.

Emotional support and anxiety reduction

When we are in uncertain, ambiguous or confusing circumstances we tend to seek the company of others in order to obtain guidance as to how to respond. In these stressful conditions we try to reduce anxiety by turning to sympathetic people who might offer information as to how to behave. In addition, people who are in a distressing situation often receive support and compassion from others.

Social comparison

There are certain situations in which we want to compare ourselves with others and affiliation provides the means of doing this. Buunk and Van Yperen (1991) found that people who are uncertain about their marriage, especially if they are unhappy with it, like to discuss this with people in a similar situation, i.e. to make social comparisons. *Social comparison theory*, formulated by Festinger (1954) and expanded by Suls and Wheeler (2000), states that people want to compare their own feelings and reactions with those of others in the same situation. This is especially true when we are in a new or fearful situation.

To gain attention

There are occasions in which we seek of the company of others in order to get attention, praise or approval. Derber (2000) argues that competition for attention is one of the most important things in a person's life. Although this is somewhat controversial, there is no doubt that people like to be valued and respected by other people and affiliation is a means by which such ambitions can be satisfied.

In everyday life we affiliate with a variety of people in order to satisfy these different motives. For example, someone who is newly diagnosed as having bowel cancer is likely to seek out experts and former sufferers who can provide both information and emotional support and thereby reduce anxiety. He or she is also likely to talk to others who have been newly diagnosed and with whom it is possible to empathise and sympathise and from whom social comparison information can be obtained. Last but not least, he or she will turn to close friends and family for emotional support during this difficult time.

Situational factors in affiliation

Our need to affiliate fluctuates across situations; there are times when we want to be with others and times when we would prefer to be alone. A survey conducted by Fox (1980) showed that people are particularly keen to be with others under pleasant conditions and under threatening ones. If we want to enjoy ourselves – for example, visit a pub, watch a football match, go to the cinema – most of us prefer to be with others rather than go alone. Our triumphs also feel better when shared ('I'm bursting to tell you – I've just passed my driving test'). Conversely, when we feel alarmed or frightened we also seek out company ('I'm not going into that house alone. My Aunt Nellie swears it's haunted').

However, there are circumstances in which we shun human contact. Fox's survey indicated that we prefer to be alone under certain unpleasant circumstances, such as when we are nervous and tense before an important interview or have just failed a test, and under conditions that require concentration, such as when we need to revise for an important test.

Research on affiliation has tended to concentrate mainly on artificial situations, usually stressful ones, in which the desire or otherwise to be with another person can be easily measured. A typical example is the often-referenced study by Schachter (1959). He induced high levels of anxiety in the experimental group of participants by leading them to expect severe, painful electric shocks during the procedure to follow. Control participants who were in the low-anxiety condition were led to expect extremely mild shocks that would merely tingle. All the participants were then asked if they would prefer to wait alone or with others. 63 per cent of those in the high-anxiety condition, as opposed to only 33 per cent in the low-anxiety condition chose to wait in the company of others, indicating that anxiety increases the need to affiliate. In later studies it was shown that, given a choice, fearful individuals chose to associate with people in the same boat (also expecting severe shocks) rather than with those who had nothing to fear. In a now classic quote, Schachter remarked that 'Misery doesn't love just any kind of company; it loves only miserable company' (Schachter, 1959, p. 24).

However, a study conducted in a more real-life situation indicated that people in stressful circumstances do not always choose to be with those expecting a similar fate. Kulik and Mahler (1989) found that cancer patients who were about to undergo an operation preferred being with people who had successfully recovered from such an operation rather than with people in a similar situation to their own. This highlights the fact that when facing an unknown threat, we turn to people who have greater experience in the hope that they can allay our fears or at least provide information.

As indicated, research on whether distressing and stressful conditions increases or decreases the desire to affiliate have led to somewhat contradictory findings. In an attempt to reconcile them, Rofé (1984) suggests that people carry out a cost/benefit analysis of the situation. Benefits include emotional support, increased safety and clarification of the situation whilst costs include embarrassment or increase in panic. Only when benefits outweigh costs do people choose to affiliate. Conversely, if costs exceed benefits people prefer to be alone. Schachter's (1959) comment is therefore not always true but depends on whether the miserable individual believes that miserable company can help them cope with the situation better than non-miserable company. In addition, when people are concerned about the possibility of increased embarrassment or negative social evaluation, they may prefer solitude to affiliation.

> ## REFLECTIVE EXERCISE 1.2
>
> Think about the situations in which you yourself prefer to be alone and those in which you prefer to be in company. Does it correspond to the research cited?

Personality factors in affiliation

Affiliation is a two-way process: because people want to affiliate, they have inbuilt behaviour patterns that encourage others to affiliate with them. When people wish to interact with other people, they use 'nonverbal immediacy behaviours': they smile, make eye contact, use an open welcoming posture, orientate their body towards the other person.

There are, however, considerable individual differences in the need to be with others and there are essential differences in the characteristics and behaviour of people who have a high need to affiliate as opposed to those who are low in this need. In general, people who are high in the need use more immediacy behaviours than those who are low in it (Mehrabian 1969). They pay more attention when interacting, appear more comfortable and generally give the impression that they are happy and relaxed in the company of others. Probably because of this, they tend to be popular. They are concerned about establishing and maintaining positive relationships with others and tend to watch other people closely in social interactions. Because they want to be accepted by others and tend to be fearful of rejection, they do sometimes show high levels of anxiety in social settings and are careful not to offend.

In this chapter it has been suggested that people have a fundamental need to belong and to form a variety of social relationships from early in life and that the first relationship with the main caregiver has a considerable influence on the personality and behaviour of the individual, particularly with reference to how they form relationships later in life. In the following chapters we look in more detail at the impact relationships have on our emotions, social behaviour and on our psychological and physical health.

Summary

- A definition of a relationship is that it exists to the extent that two people exert strong, frequent and diverse effects on one another over an extended period of time.
- The main theoretical perspectives from which relationships are viewed are reinforcement theories, evolutionary psychology and attachment theory. They are not mutually exclusive.
- Baumeister and Leary (1995) argue that humans have an innate 'need to belong'. This has evolved because group living helps us survive, reproduce and rear offspring to maturity.
- Human infants have an innate need to attach. The type of attachment a child has early in life acts as an internal working model for all later social relationships. If this does not happen satisfactorily and the child is insecurely attached or fails to attach, there are long-term deleterious consequences including the inability to form meaningful long-term relationships.
- Infants have a complex array of innate behaviours that enable them to make relationships. These include face recognition, differentiating between familiar and unfamiliar faces, empathic accuracy, and verbal and non-verbal communication.
- Humans also have an innate tendency to affiliate, that is, to interact with other people. Hill (1987) suggests several motives for mixing with others including the innate enjoyment of others' company, obtaining emotional support, anxiety reduction, making social comparison and to gain attention. The need to affiliate varies across situations: in some circumstances we want to be alone, but in others, we feel the need to be with other people.

FURTHER READING

Baumeister, R.F. & Leary, M.R. (1995) The need to belong: Desire for interpersonal attachments as a fundamental human motivation. *Psychological Bulletin*, *117*, 497–529.

Bowlby, J. (1988) *A Secure Base: Clinical Applications of Attachment Theory*. London: Routledge.

Caporael, L.R. (2007) Evolutionary theory for social and cultural psychology. In A.W. Kruglanski & E. Tory Higgins (Eds.), *Social Psychology: Handbook of Basic Principles* (2nd edn). New York: Guilford Press.

FURTHER READING

Methodology in relationship research

2

What this chapter will teach you

- How research is conducted to describe behaviour in relationships: observations, surveys and social neuroscience.

- How research is conducted to see if there is an association between variables in relationships: correlations.

- How research is conducted to establish cause and effect in relationships: experimental methods.

- The problem of selection of participants in research on relationships.

When studying interpersonal relationships, researchers are interested in trying to answer many types of questions. Why do we like some people and not others? What happens when we fall in love? What factors contribute to a successful marriage? What *is* a 'successful' marriage? How often do relatives keep in touch with each other? Can a relationship have an effect on your health? If so, how?

Since the list of questions is so extensive and the topic areas so diverse, no single method will provide all the answers: our understanding of this area depends on the gradual accumulation of knowledge gleaned by many researchers looking at the same aspects of relationships in different ways.

Formulating a testable research question/hypothesis

The first stage in trying to answer any questions in this research field (or any other) is to formulate the question in such a way that it is a *testable research question* or *hypothesis*. The nature of the question posed determines the method chosen. We can, for convenience sake, divide the type of research interest into three broad categories:

- Describing behaviour.
- Looking at an association between variables.
- Investigating causal relationships.

1 When a researcher is interested in *describing behaviour* (e.g. how fathers and pre-school children interact during a shopping trip; how people act on their first date), then a variety of descriptive methods is available including *observational methods* and *survey research*.

2 If the focus of attention is whether there is an *association between variables* (e.g. is there an association between amount of social support and good health; do friends have similar interests?) then a *correlation* is a suitable choice.

3 Should the researcher wish to establish whether there is *causal relationship* between variables (e.g. is our liking for an individual influenced by how good-looking they are?), then the *experimental method* must be used.

Data collection

In addition to different methods, there is also a variety of ways in which data can be collected (content analysis, self-report, use of rating scales, the diary method). These will be discussed within the context of the methods themselves.

Descriptive research

Observational methods

When researchers simply want to describe behaviour (for example, what friends talk about when they meet up, the posture and body movements of couples, the flirting behaviour of teenagers), then one option is to use an observational method. There are various types of observation.

A **naturalistic observation study** involves detailed observations of participants in a real-life setting. Dunn and Munn (1986) used this method to look specifically at the frequency of sharing, helping, comforting and cooperative behaviour shown by young siblings towards one another, their response to the other child's distress, and the relation between this pro-social behaviour and conflict behaviour.

A **structured observation** involves looking at behaviour in a particular situation that has been carefully set up by the investigator and is the same for all the participants. Ainsworth, in a series of studies (known as the Strange Situation studies), used this method to observe the behaviour of infants when their main caregiver left them in an unfamiliar place and then returned (e.g. Ainsworth *et al.* 1978 – see Chapter 1).

Observations in psychology should be *objective* and systematic in order to try and reduce the possibilities of error and bias. This is done by ensuring that all observers watch the same behaviour and measure

Figure 2.1 Naturalistic observation involves observing people in a natural setting.

it in the same way. It is necessary, therefore, for observers to have a clear idea of exactly what they are observing and to use a system for categorising and recording information. In many circumstances it is impossible to observe everyone all of the time, so observers use various techniques to sample behaviour. The two commonest of these are time sampling (e.g. observing for 1 minute every 5 minutes) and event sampling – counting the number of times a certain behaviour occurs in a group of individuals.

There should be careful training of observers and at least two of them to record behaviour in order to establish good *inter-observer reliability* (sometimes called inter-rater reliability), i.e. good agreement between them. Nevertheless, maintaining reliability can be problematic since there is always liable to be some subjectivity in the way the observers interpret behaviour.

With respect to measuring the behaviour, typically the interaction between people would be videotaped and a *content analysis* done on the raw data using a carefully constructed behaviour coding system. *Behaviour coding* systems consist of a set of carefully defined codes that researchers use to label or rate behaviour as they observe and code it. Each behavioural coding system is unique, depending on what is of interest to researchers about the interactions they will be observing. One of the most popular coding systems is the Specific Affect Coding System (SPAFF), which is most frequently used to code problem-solving interactions with couples, but is also used to code many other interactions. Behaviour is recorded on video and then coded second-by-second; typical behaviours that are coded are facial expression and the content and context of speech. Researchers using this system can identify both warning signs of relationship distress as well as highlight strengths of satisfied couples; the information can have important application in identifying the health of a relationship and suggesting means of improving it. Importantly, behavioural coding provides researchers with information about not only each unique interaction, but also with a standard by which they can compare behaviour across entire samples.

Naturalistic observation has high *ecological validity*, that is, the results do generalise to the real world. Structured observations have less ecological validity but they do allow researchers to observe events that may not occur very often in a natural setting but are of importance in everyday experiences (it is, for example, useful to know how children react to separation experiences). An additional advantage is that because the set-up is the same for all participants, it allows comparison to be made between individuals and results can be generalised.

Surveys

Surveys involve designing and administering a *questionnaire* in order to obtain specific information about beliefs, attitudes, behaviour and so on from a certain sample of the population. Fox (1980) used a survey to ascertain the circumstances under which people prefer to be with others as compared to those in which they prefer to be alone (ch. 1) whilst Straus *et al.* (1980) used it to investigate the amount of violence in American families. Surveys require a measuring instrument; for example, Straus used the Conflict Tactics Scale (CTS) (Straus, 1979, 1990) to ascertain the incidence of both minor and major violence within families.

One common method of measuring attitudes is to use a **Likert Scale**. This involves giving the respondents a series of attitude statements and asking them to rate them according to their degree of agreement. There are usually five levels: strongly agree, agree, uncertain, disagree, strongly disagree. Some scales use seven or even more choices and some omit the neutral/uncertain element. These scales are useful because the scores can be analysed easily and the opinion questionnaires are fairly quick to complete, so a large number of attitudes can be easily collected. The obvious disadvantage is that they do not allow for any detailed opinions to be expressed.

> **KEY TERMS**
>
> **Survey** A method that involves designing and administering questionnaires in order to obtain specific information about beliefs, attitudes and behaviour.
>
> **Likert Scale** A scale used mainly to measure attitudes. It consists of a series of attitude statements with which the respondent has to express the extent of agreement from a fixed choice of statements. The most common is a 5-point scale ranging from *strongly agree* to *strongly disagree*, although other scales can be used.

Figure 2.2 Likert Scales measure the extent of agreement/disagreement with an opinion statement.

RESEARCH EXERCISE

Buunk and Van Yperen (1991) measured marital satisfaction using a Likert scale (see Chapter 4). Go to http://www.elainehatfield.com/120.pdf to look at Likert scales measuring equity in relationships.

Any self-report method has the advantage that information is obtained direct from the participant rather than from an outside observer. Nevertheless, there are various issues that need to be addressed when using surveys.

A major problem is that in such self-report methods there is *bias* in participants' reports. One such is the *social desirability bias* in which, in order to put themselves in a favourable light, people do not necessarily tell the truth, especially on sensitive topics. Another such bias that distorts the truth is the *egocentric bias* in which we see the world from our own perspective which may not be objective. One example of this to which we may all relate is the fact that people tend to overestimate the amount of domestic chores they do and underestimate those of their partner!

There may also be *problems of memory*, especially if the questionnaire involves recalling events that happened some years ago (questionnaire items such as 'what feelings did you experience during your first kiss?'). *Interpretation* is yet another issue, since participants may misunderstand the question that is asked. One example reported by Brehm (1992) comes from a study by Berger and Wenger (1973) in which some participants accepted 'she brings herself to climax' as a possible definition of loss of virginity in a woman!

Sampling bias is a significant problem of the survey method; indeed one of the greatest challenges when conducting surveys is how to obtain an appropriate sample of participants. Many of the target population may decline to take part and non-respondents may differ from those who are willing to respond in significant ways. For example, those people who are extremely violent towards their families are far less likely to agree to participate in a survey on the topic than those who use moderate or nonviolent means of coercion.

Nowadays many surveys are conducted online and this brings with it a new set of advantages and problems. One obvious advantage is that the researcher has access to a wide variety of individuals and groups who would be difficult, if not impossible, to reach through other means since many groups only exist in cyberspace. Discussion forums provide the researcher with access to participants who share specific interests, attitudes, beliefs and values and/or demographic characteristics (e.g. groups of older people; those looking for a partner; those experiencing problems with children). Other advantages include automated data collection that reduces time, effort and costs. On the negative side, online surveys suffer their own sampling problems. Relatively little may be known about the characteristics of people in online communities; in addition, not all members of virtual groups allow their email addresses to be listed, so such lists are not representative of the online community.

Levine *et al.* (1995) conducted a survey to assess beliefs about the importance of love in marriage, an issue discussed in Chapter 7. The questionnaire used was originally used by Kephart (1967) and Simpson *et al.* (1986). It consisted of just three questions:

> ## RESEARCH QUESTION
>
> In what ways do you think the members of online groups who allow their email addresses to be listed may differ from those who keep them confidential? How might the sample of participants selected for an online survey from a virtual discussion group be non-representative?

1   If a man (woman) had all the other qualities you desired, would you marry this person if you were not in love with him (her). (Yes, no, or undecided).
2   If love has completely disappeared from a marriage, I think it is probably best for the couple to make a clean break and start new lives. (Agree, disagree, or neutral).
3   In my opinion, the disappearance of love is not sufficient reason for ending a marriage and should not be viewed as such (agree, disagree, or neutral).

For each of these questions, the respondent answers 'no', 'yes' or 'undecided'. It is easy to provide a score for each participant and then analyse the total scores in terms of gender differences, cultural differences and differences over time. One interesting finding is that the percentage of people willing to contemplate marrying a person they are not in love with (question 1) decreased markedly from 1967 to 1986.

Social neuroscience

Social neuroscience has provided another means by which to collect descriptive data (which may or may not be used to then investigate associations or causal relationships). Social neuroscience is a fairly new branch of psychology devoted to understanding how biological systems implement social behaviour and how, in turn, social behaviour impacts on the brain and biology. It is concerned with the neural mechanisms that underlie our behaviour, explains our ability to recognise, understand and interact

> ### KEY TERM
>
> **Social neuroscience** A fairly new branch of psychology devoted to understanding how biological systems implement social behaviour and how, in turn, social behaviour impacts on the brain and biology.

with others. A number of methods are used in social neuroscience including functional magnetic resonance imaging (fMRI) and other brain scanning techniques, galvanic skin response (GSR), endocrinology, and the collection of physiological data such as levels of stress hormones in blood.

Research into associations

Correlations

KEY TERM

Correlation A method of establishing whether there is an association (relationship) between two variables. A correlation is positive when both variables increase or decrease together; it is negative when, as one increases, the other decreases.

The method of **correlation** looks at whether there is an association between two variables, for example, whether there is an association between the amount of attitude similarity between pairs of friends and the degree of satisfaction with the friendship. If researchers find that greater attitude similarity is associated with greater relationship satisfaction, there is a *positive correlation* between the two variables. A positive correlation means that high values of one variable are associated with high values of the other (and that low values of one are associated with low values of the other). In our example, this means that the more similar people are in their attitudes, the more satisfying they find the relationship.

An example of a positive correlation is given in Chapter 3. Feingold (1988) found a high positive correlation for interpersonal attractiveness in dating couples across a wide range of studies: in other words, a good looking person is likely to date another good-looker; the converse also being true. An older study by Silverman (1971) is interesting because data was collected in the field (in real-life situations) by assessing the attractiveness of each of a pair of dating couples. This data was then analysed using a correlation; again, a positive correlation was found. More recently, Taylor *et al.* (2011) used data from an online dating site (as well as the laboratory) for a similar analysis.

A correlation may also be negative, in which case high values of one variable are associated with low levels of another. An example of a negative correlation is given in Chapter 9: Dainton and Aylor (2011) found that the *more* uncertain an individual was in a relationship, the *less* they used so-called maintenance behaviours (such as being positive and giving assurances) in their romantic relationship.

Zero correlation means that there is no association between two variables. Although often considered by laypersons to be an unimportant finding, the lack of a correlation between variables can be of considerable use in relationship research.

Correlations not only vary in whether they are positive, negative or neutral but in their strength. Numerically they vary from a 'perfect' positive correlation of +1 through zero to a 'perfect' negative correlation of −1.

Establishing whether or not an association exists between variables is a useful piece of information in itself and can be used as the basis for further investigations. It also has considerable predictive value: if an association exists between variables, such as the degree to which two people are physically attractive, then we can generally predict that in the future, most romantic couples will pair according to this trend with very attractive people pairing with very attractive partners. Obviously there will be exceptions, but the general trend will continue to be in that direction.

Laurenceau *et al.* (2005) asked married couples to keep daily diary accounts of their interactions and found that the intimacy in a relationship could be predicted from the amount of self-disclosure and partner disclosure (see Chapter 8). The diary method is particularly useful here because it reflects the actual daily accounts of what happens in the couple's daily lives, so it has high ecological validity. It does not depend on retrospective data (looking back), which could be inaccurate. Of course, it does depend on the couples being vigilant in keeping the diaries and not neglecting to mention unpleasant as well as pleasant interactions.

The main disadvantage with the correlational designs is that it cannot tell us whether or not one variable *causes* another, and we are left with several unanswered questions about the reasons for the association. Take the example that there is a positive correlation between the degree in attitude similarity and the level of satisfaction in friendships. Do people choose friends because they have similar attitudes to themselves? This implies that attitude similarity *causes* friendship satisfaction. Alternatively, are people first attracted to someone and then, the more they like someone, the more they change their attitudes to match theirs? In this case, the implication is that friendship satisfaction *causes* attitude similarity. Yet another possibility is that people make friends with those from similar backgrounds because they are the people they meet in the course of their everyday lives, and people from similar backgrounds tend both to like each other and share similar attitudes. Unlike the first two possibilities, this one implies no direct cause and effect between the two variables but a third factor (similar background) that influences both of the other two.

Unfortunately, many people misinterpret the findings of correlational studies and jump to conclusions about cause and effect. This is well worth bearing in mind when you consider the research studies discussed in this text.

Correlations allow us to look at real-life variables, such as love, sexual behaviour and commitment. This means that this method is likely to have high **ecological validity**, that is, it can sample behaviour that exists in real-life situations but, with no apology for the repetition, they do not permit conclusions about cause and effect.

Research into causation

Experiments

The experimental method is the research tool that is ideally suited to establishing cause and effect and was a popular method in early relationship research. An example of such a method was used by Byrne (see Chapter 3) in a series of studies to see if perceived attitude similarity affected degree of liking. Participants were shown a profile of an individual and asked to estimate how much they were attracted to that individual. The degree of similarity to the participant had been systematically varied to see if it affecting liking. The variable that has been manipulated is the *independent variable* (in this case, the extent of attitude similarity) and the one being measured is the *dependent variable* (in this case, the degree of liking).

In essence, an experiment involves the systematic manipulation of an independent variable in order to measure its effect on a dependent variable. However, there are other variables that might have an effect on the dependent variable and these are known as confounding variables. If, in the example above, the individual described not only differed in attitude similarity but in age, then age would be a confounding variable. The control of confounding variables is a tricky business because there are many potential variables. The usual controls are to ensure that the participants are randomly assigned to the different conditions and that the procedure is well controlled so each participant is treated in an identical manner (they receive the same instructions, they are tested by the same researcher in the same room and so on).

The major advantage of the experimental method is that it allows us to establish cause and effect. In our example we can see if attitude similarity *causes* liking. There are, however, many limitations to this design, especially with regard to research in interpersonal relationships. The major drawback is that of lack of ecological validity. We cannot truly mimic how people relate to each other in real life. For example, everyday experiences of meeting someone new do not usually involve seeing a profile of them first and then consciously rating how we feel about them. Laboratory situations can never truly reflect the important factors in intimate relationships. For practical reasons we cannot, and for ethical reasons we should not, create love, jealousy and passion in the laboratory. Whereas this does mean that laboratory experiments are limited in that they can only really investigate fairly detached, emotionless interactions between strangers, nevertheless, the experimental method does give useful information on some limited aspects of relationship development especially in their very early stages.

Selection of participants

A problem with which all researchers in psychology are faced is the selection of participants to take part in investigations. In an ideal world, we would look in detail at a large and representative sample of the population, drawn from all sorts of walks of life – people of all ages, from a wide variety of cultural and socioeconomic backgrounds. Unfortunately, obtaining such a sample is difficult and expensive. A commonly used sampling method employed by researchers, especially in the early research is to draw on those people who are readily available, such as students. Such an *opportunity sample* (or convenience sample) means that invariably the sample consists of a very narrow range of participants in terms of age, educational and socioeconomic status and cultural background. What we must bear in mind is that, in any psychological investigation, the results obtained only apply to people who have the same characteristics as the participants.

In addition to this, when investigating a very large number of people, it is impractical to obtain really detailed information from them. If, for example, a wide-scale survey were to be conducted, only a limited amount of information could be obtained from each participant. It is only feasible to obtain in-depth information from a relatively small number of participants and this, in turn, makes generalisation difficult.

RESEARCH QUESTION

In this book there are several examples of studies being criticised on the grounds of using a biased sample, often college students. Make a list of these as you go along so they can be used in essays or in the introduction/discussion section of your own coursework if it is based on these studies.

Summary

- The first stage in conducting research is to formulate a testable question or hypothesis. Research interests can be classified into three groups:
    o Describing behaviour.
    o Investigating an association between variables.
    o Investigating causal relationships.
- Descriptive research may use observational methods, surveys and social neuroscience as a means of collecting data. With respect to observations:
    o A naturalistic observation study involves detailed observations of people in an everyday setting.
    o A structured observation involves looking at people in a particular situation that has been manipulated by the researcher so it is identical for every participant.
    o Observations should be objective and systematic in order to reduce error and bias. There should be good inter-observer reliability.
    o Naturalistic observations have high ecological validity but are not necessarily generalisable. Structured observations have lower ecological validity but allow results to be generalised to other similar groups of individuals.
- Surveys involve designing and administering question-naires in order to obtain specific information about beliefs, attitudes and behaviour.
    o They are often scored using a Likert scale.
    o They allow researchers to obtain a large amount of data on a specific topic quickly and easily.
    o There are problems of the accuracy of the answers and of obtaining a representative sample of participants.
- The method of correlation involves looking at whether there is an association between two variables.
    o Correlations allow predictions to be made: if there is a high correlation between two variables (whether positive or negative) and one variable is known, the other can be predicted.
    o Correlations only show the extent of an association between variables; they do not show cause and effect.

- The experimental method allows conclusions to be drawn about cause and effect. An experiment involves the manipulation of an independent variable in order to measure its effect on a dependent variable whilst keeping all other variables constant.
  - o The experimental method has the advantage that it establishes cause and effect (and is the only method by which this can be done).
  - o The main disadvantage of the experimental method is a lack of ecological validity due to the fact that they are often carried out in artificial situations and do not investigate aspects of long-term real-life relationships.
- Selection of participants can be a problem in relationship research. Many studies use an opportunity sample consisting of a narrow range participants in terms of age, educational and socioeconomic status and cultural background.

FURTHER READING

Regan, P. (2011). *Close Relationships* (Chapter 2). New York: Routledge.

Determinants of interpersonal attraction

3

What this chapter will teach you

- The main factors that determine with whom we make friends and form romantic relationships.

- Why each of these factors is important.

- Whether opposites attract or birds of a feather flock together.

- Whether the internet has changed the way in which relationships are formed.

In our everyday lives we meet a multitude of people but only form lasting relationships with a few. On what basis do we choose our friends and romantic partners? In this chapter, we consider research findings into the factors that help determine the onset of friendship or romance and the reasons why these factors may be influential.

Proximity

Proximity is a powerful force in interpersonal attraction; indeed probably the best predictor of whether two people will become friends is how far apart they are. Because of where people live, sit in a classroom or earn a living they have close contact with particular people, and it is this physical arrangement that is hugely influential in determining friendship patterns.

In a classic study, Festinger *et al.* (1950) observed the friendships that formed in a block of apartments for married students consisting of seventeen separate buildings, each comprising ten flats on two floors. More than ten times as many friendships formed between students who shared the same building than between students in different ones. Within the same building, friendships were far more likely between people who lived on the same floor than between those on different floors.

It was not only physical distance that made a difference: the most popular people were those who had apartments nearest the staircases and postboxes. This indicates that the **functional distance**, that is, the likelihood of two people coming into contact, is also very influential. In fact, as this study demonstrates, architectural features can significantly affect the likelihood that people will make friends. Those who live in apartments or rooms not often passed by others are liable to make far fewer friends than those who live near communal areas such as shared bathrooms, kitchens, lounges and stairways. People allocated rooms at the end of a corridor, away from the main thoroughfares, may initially welcome the privacy and peace this offers, but may eventually feel isolated and lonely. This also applies on housing estates: those living at the end of a cul-de-sac are likely to have fewer friends in the immediate locality than those whose houses are situated on busy intersections.

> **KEY TERM**
>
> **Functional distance** The smaller the functional distance between two people, the greater the likelihood that two people will interact. This is more influential than the actual distance in friendship formation.

Several other studies support the importance of both physical distance and functional distance in friendship formation. Segal (1974) monitored the friendship patterns of police cadets who were assigned to their rooms and to seats in classrooms according to the alphabetical order of their surname. He found that friendships tended to form between people whose surnames were close in the alphabet. Hogg and Tindale (2001) also demonstrated that assignment to the same work unit increases the likelihood of becoming friends. Yinin *et al.* (1977) compared friendships in Israeli dormitories that differed in the amount of interaction they permitted. In some dormitories students had their own *en-suite* facilities and had little cause to interact. In others, the toilets, showers and kitchens were all shared, resulting in high interaction. The higher the level of interaction, the higher the proportion of friends chosen from within the living unit.

This pattern does not just apply to youth. Nehamow and Lawton (1975) found that of the friendships between elderly people living in an urban housing complex, 88 per cent were formed by those living in the same building.

Neither does it apply simply to friendship: love tends to blossom at close quarters. Bossard (1932) examined the premarital addresses of the first 5,000 couples married in one city in 1931. More than half of the couples had lived within short walking distance of each other. Similar studies conducted around the same time in other cities confirm these findings.

Proximity also seems to triumph over similarity. In a significant study, Deutsch and Collins (1951) found that when people were assigned to rented public housing without regard to their race, many interracial friendships developed among the residents.

The distance between people is also an important factor in the significance of interpersonal interactions. Latané et al. (1995) found that the great majority of 'memorable interactions' (those involving topics of personal importance) were conducted with people living less than a mile away, with only 10 per cent at a distance greater than 50 miles.

The obvious question (which I daresay the reader has anticipated) is whether things have changed in these days of the internet. One would expect that, in an era in which it is almost as easy to communicate across the globe as it is across the street, we would see what Frances Cairncross refers to as 'The Death of Distance' (Cairncross 1997). This does not, however, appear to be the case. Whilst the advent of the internet and technologies such as the mobile phone have obviously had an effect on relationships (see Chapter 6), the formation of friendships appears still to be very dependent on the physical distance between individuals. Although the picture is complex, it is fair to say that most friendships are still initiated offline. Lenhart and Madden (2007) found that most online friends are still local, and social networking sites are used to strengthen existing friendships rather than to form them. Even in online exchanges, with the exception of email, the frequency of contact is strongly related to distance (Mok & Wellman 2007). As Mok et al. (2008) comment 'the frequency of face-to-face contact among socially-close friends and relatives has hardly changed between the 1970s and the 2000s'. In a nutshell, distance does still matter – it's hard to hug online!

REFLECTIVE EXERCISE 3.1

See if the findings of Lenhart and Madden (2007) apply to you (there is more similar research in Chapter 6). Are most of your online friends those people with whom you were already friendly? In your opinion, what effect has social media had on your own relationships? Has it strengthened existing friendships; allowed you to keep in touch with people with whom you wouldn't otherwise have bothered; allowed you to make friends you've never met (or had not met when the friendship was initiated)?

A small project invites! A survey of people of various ages to see how the internet has affected their relationships. The type of social media sites people of different ages use (if any). How these sites are used. Lots of similar possibilities.

There are, however, exceptions to the general rule that close proximity predicts increased liking. Some people may be only too aware that neighbours can be sworn enemies rather than friends. Ebbesen *et al.* (1976) point out that not all neighbourhoods, even if they are fairly homogeneous, are occupied by people who like each other. They argue that a person might dislike another who lives near them due to 'environmental spoiling': a car parked in an inconsiderate place, music played too loudly and so on. This environmental-spoiling hypothesis implies that dislike may not require face-to-face contact but it does require close proximity. Paradoxically, the formation of enemies is even more dependent on physical proximity than is the formation of friendships.

A second limitation to the general rule is that when we encounter people too frequently we may become bored with them and tire of the relationship (Bornstein *et al.* 1990; Norton *et al.* 2007).

Why is proximity important?

There are several reasons why the physical or functional distance between two people will predict friendship.

Familiarity

Many researchers believe that the reason we like those people whom we see most often is because they are familiar to us. Zajonc (1968, 2001) argues that *mere exposure* to someone is sufficient to make us like them, as has been demonstrated in many research studies (e.g. Harmon-Jones & Allen 2001). There are several suggestions as to why familiarity should increase liking. As we saw in the first chapter, evolutionary psychologists have speculated that it makes evolutionary sense to be innately wary of the unfamiliar because strangers and unfamiliar objects may represent a threat whilst familiar people and things may be reassuring. Another suggestion is that familiarity increases predictability, which is, in turn, comforting. A third possibility is that the more familiar we are with someone, the more similar we perceive them to be. As we shall see in the next section, similarity is very important in interpersonal attraction. (However, it's worth noting that there is a school of thought that argues that familiarity breeds contempt; see Norton *et al.* 2007).

Low costs

It takes little time or effort to interact with someone whom you meet on a regular basis and this gives you more opportunity to get to know them. The more you see someone, the more opportunity you have to discover mutual interests. Conversely, long distance relationships take a lot of effort in terms of time, money and planning. No matter how much close friends swear to stay in touch when they move apart, these relationships often dwindle to the occasional phone call and email because they are costly to maintain in terms of effort.

Expectation of continued interaction

When we expect to encounter people on a regular basis, and we cannot avoid them (at work, for instance), we try harder to see the good side of these people. We tend to exaggerate their positive points and minimise their negative ones. Given that they are likely to react in the same way, friendship becomes very probable.

Predictability

Within reason, we prefer our environment to be predictable. When people are unpredictable we feel nervous, anxious and uncomfortable; when they are predictable we feel safe and relaxed. Note the caveat *within reason*: if people are too predictable, they simply become boring.

Similarity

'Birds of a feather flock together' is a well-known saying that has a considerable ring of truth to it: research indicates that friends and lovers tend to be similar in demography, in attitudes and values and in personality. Berscheid and Reis (1998) argue that similarity is one of most well-established findings in the study of interpersonal attraction.

Early research, albeit rather artificial, confirmed the importance of similarity. For example, Byrne and his colleagues conducted many laboratory studies in which participants were requested to complete a questionnaire concerning their personal characteristics (e.g. Byrne 1971; Byrne *et al.* 1971). They were then shown the questionnaire answers of another person and asked about their personal feelings towards this stranger. The questionnaires shown to the participants were, in fact, fabricated ones, manipulated to adjust the degree of similarity between that of the bogus (invented) person and the participant. From the results of these so-called 'bogus stranger' studies, Byrne (1971) formulated the *law of attraction*, which states that there is a direct linear relationship between the level of attraction and the proportion of similar attitudes.

Field studies confirm the importance of similarity. Kendel (1978) analysed the friendship patterns of more than 1,800 adolescents between the ages of 13 and 18 and found that 'best' friends were similar in terms of age, religion, ethnic group and family income and that they shared the same leisure interests. Kupersmidt *et al.* (1995) found that in both primary and senior schools, friends were similar in age and academic achievement as well as patterns of aggressive behaviour and social withdrawal. When college students are randomly assigned to be roommates, it is the most similar couples in terms of personality who are most likely to form lasting friendships (Carli *et al.* 1991).

AhYun (2002) demonstrated that similarity of attitudes, interests and values, as well as age, marital status and ethnic background, influences the development of friendships. Batool and Malik (2010), investigating same-gender friends from Punjab, Pakistan, found that similarity was the main factor in interpersonal attraction and was equally important for both men and women. These researchers also considered the relative influence of proximity and similarity. They point out that in some cases proximity can lead to dislike of an individual, but as long as proximity makes people aware of their similarity, increased proximity enhances liking. In essence, once people establish that they are similar, proximity increases that attraction. The deepest friendships are between similar people who live close to one another.

Similarity effects are not only true of positive characteristics: antisocial individuals tend to be attracted to one another (Krueger *et al.* 1998) as do depressives (Locke & Horowitz 1990). In a wittily entitled study, 'How do I love thee? Let me count the Js', Jones *et al.* (2004) found there is even evidence that similarity of letters in a person's names increases attractiveness!

Romantic partners as well as friends also tend to be matched in terms of a host of variables. For example, Hill and Peplau (1998) found that dating couples tend to be alike in age, intelligence, educational attainment, religion and physical attractiveness. Furthermore, couples who were similar at the start of the study were the most likely to be together 1 year and 15 years later.

Similarity of physical attractiveness has received particular attention. Walster *et al.* (1966) proposed a **matching hypothesis**, which states that in the initial stages of a romantic relationship, people tend to choose a partner of roughly equal social desirability. Several studies have looked at the physical attractiveness ratings of newly-weds or dating couples and found that each member of the pair tends to be similar in level of attractiveness.

KEY TERM

The matching hypothesis People tend to form romantic relationships or friendships with those of a similar level of physical attractiveness to themselves.

In a meta-analysis of 17 studies, Feingold (1988) found a high positive correlation for interpersonal attractiveness in dating couples. Silverman (1971) conducted a field study in which researchers observed couples in bars and similar places and found, as expected, that they shared similar levels of attractiveness. Taylor *et al.* (2011), using data collected from the laboratory and from a popular online dating site, found evidence for matching based on physical attractiveness, as well as popularity and self-worth. This means that, despite the fact that people doubtless 'fancy' those with drop dead gorgeous looks who are out of their league, realism comes into play and most people form a romantic liaison with someone of equal physical attractiveness (Burley 1983).

Perhaps more surprisingly, matching on physical attractiveness tends to apply to friendships as well as romantic relationships (Feingold 1988). In a field study, McKillip and Riedel (1983) observed pairs in real-life settings such as bars, assessed each on level of attraction and then asked them whether they were friends or lovers. If they were lovers they were then asked how strong and committed was their relationship. Both friends and lovers tended to be matched on physical attractiveness but the more casual lovers were less likely than the committed ones to be closely matched.

The relationship between attraction and similarity is fairly robust, but there are exceptions. If individuals have very low self-esteem, so that they don't like themselves very much, then neither do they like those whom they perceive as being similar to them (Leonard 1975).

Complementarity

What about the saying 'opposites attract'? Do research findings on the prevalence of similarity completely deny its veracity? In popular culture, there is a notion that individuals are attracted to people whose characteristics are different but complementary to their own. This is based on the belief that opposites attract because it allows them to divide tasks and pursue goals without too much disagreement. The most obvious example is that if one of couple enjoys staying home raising children while the other prefers to earn money outside the home, then this can be achieved without conflict. On the whole there is little support for this contention (Markey & Markey 2009; O'Leary & Smith, 1991) and this type of complementarity is neither sought by partners nor does it lead to long-term harmony, especially among romantic couples. Nevertheless, there is evidence of complementarity when it comes to dominance and submission: Markey and Markey (2007), investigating couples who had been dating at least a year, found that those who reported the greatest satisfaction were those who were similar in warmth but dissimilar in terms of dominance: on this dimension there is probably more evidence of complementarity than similarity. (But there are some interesting exceptions such as lesbian relationships; see Markey & Markey 2011.) This supports the interpersonal complementarity model (Carson 1969) which holds that the most compatible romantic couples are those who are similar on warmth but opposite on dominance.

The means by which similarity affects relationship formation has been a source of interest and argument in social psychology. Although research shows a correlational relationship between similarity and friendship, it does not necessarily mean that we are attracted to another person *because* they are similar to us. Rosenbaum (1986) contends that social psychologists have overestimated the role of similarity of attitudes in interpersonal relations. In his **repulsion hypothesis**, he argues that we don't necessarily like people who share our attitudes but we do dislike those whose attitudes differ greatly from ours. When we choose a long-term partner, we first eliminate all those whose attitudes contrast with our own and then select more or less randomly from the remainder. According to this hypothesis, it is not so much that there a similarity-attraction effect but more of a dissimilarity-repulsion effect.

There is not a great deal of research evidence in support of this contention. Smeaton *et al.* (1989) kept the number of dissimilar attitudes of a bogus stranger the same but varied the number of similar attitudes. They found that, contrary to the repulsion hypothesis, the proportion of similar attitudes did have an effect. Nevertheless, Rosenbaum's contention has been of value in focusing attention on the influence of attitude dissimilarity. Evidence does indicate that disparate attitudes do have a slightly greater effect than do similar attitudes (Chapman 1992).

Byrne *et al.* (1986) suggest, in their *proportional hypothesis*, a two-stage process in which the first stage is the same as that suggested by the repulsion hypothesis but the second stage differs. They propose that when we meet someone new we initially reject as potential friends all those who have very dissimilar attitudes to our own and from the remainder we select as friends those people with whom we share similar attitudes.

REFLECTIVE EXERCISE 3.2

You may wish to read the article by Markey and Markey (2011) and consider why lesbian relationships may be an exception to the dominance/submissive 'rule'.

KEY TERM

Repulsion hypothesis We dislike those people whose attitudes are very different from our own; similarity of attitudes is irrelevant.

Why is similarity important?

- Byrne (1971) argues that people who agree with our attitudes bolster our self-esteem by making our own view of the world appear accurate, reasonable and worthy of respect.
- There is a general assumption that people similar to us will like us. Since there are few things quite as rewarding as being liked by others, we are attracted to similar others in anticipation of this reward.
- It is easier to communicate with people who are similar to us. Being with them gives us a feeling of unity and a sense of belonging. We can relax and enjoy their company. We also anticipate that future meetings will be enjoyable and free from anxiety and conflict.

Physical attraction

To quote from a novel by David Lodge, 'Blessed are the good looking for they shall have fun'. There is little doubt that, no matter how unfair it is and how much we try to resist it, being physically attractive has huge advantages. Beauty greatly improves a person's popularity both in sexual relationships and in friendships.

A classic study by Walster *et al.* (1966) established the importance of physical attraction. They conducted a huge 'blind date' investigation in which, for one evening, male and female students were paired randomly and later asked to rate their date on various measures. It was found that characteristics such as personality, intelligence, interests and self-esteem made little difference to the ratings. The only significant predictor of how highly people were rated was their physical attractiveness.

DISCUSS AND DEBATE

Ethics

Read the classic 'blind date' study by Walster *et al.* (1966) – it is in many textbooks including, in some detail, Dwyer (2000). Consider the several ethical issues that are raised by this study including deception of various kinds (including the secret rating of the participants on attractiveness), and no fully informed consent. Some of the questions asked of the participants – how much they liked their date, how attractive they found them and so on – also raise ethical questions. To what extent do you think they are justified? On what grounds do you make your judgements? (Does the research tell us anything we did not already know? Are the findings important to society?)

KEY TERM

The halo effect People who are judged positively in one attribute are also judged positively in others. In relationships, this is most often used to explain the fact that people who are physically attractively are considered to have other positive characteristics such as being intelligent, kind, loving and competent.

A great deal of subsequent research in many cultures has consistently confirmed that beauty enhances social life (Langlois *et al*. 2000; Eastwick & Finkel 2008). Beautiful people are also assumed to have other positive characteristics, the so-called **halo effect**, that people who are judged positively on one characteristic are also judged positively on others. Physically attractive individuals are seen as more socially competent than those that are physically unattractive; they are also regarded as more intelligent, well-adjusted, and self-assertive (Eagly *et al*. 1991) as well as more competent (Jackson *et al*. 1995). Compared to attractive individuals, unattractive individuals are seen as unhealthy, unpopular and unintelligent (Lundberg & Sheehan 1994).

In 11 meta-analyses, Langlois *et al*. (2000) found that attractive children and adults are judged and treated more positively than unattractive children and adults even by those who know them. Attractive individuals are more likely to receive help, be accepted by others or be recommended for a job. The effect is extremely pervasive: even young children prefer their physically attractive peers and consider that unattractive children are unfriendly and aggressive (Dion & Berscheid 1974).

Nevertheless, although attractive people are generally more popular, extreme beauty can have its disadvantages. Exceptionally attractive people tend to have fewer than average same-sex friends and are

Figure 3.1 'Butter wouldn't melt....' attractive children are judged more leniently than unattractive children.

liable to be judged vain, self-centred and unsympathetic (Dermer & Thiel 1975). The ideal is to be very attractive but not exceptionally so (chance would be a fine thing!).

Why is physical attraction important?

- As already noted, there is an assumption that beautiful people have other good qualities as well; the stereotype of 'what is beautiful is good' is well entrenched (Eagly *et al.* 1991). It is therefore assumed that the company of attractive individuals is likely to be stimulating and fun.
- We may benefit from what has been called 'the radiating effect of beauty': we gain considerable prestige from being associated with and 'chosen' by a glamorous companion, even when the relationship is not a romantic one. Research indicates that both men and women are rated more favourably when they are accompanied by an attractive partner or friend than when they have an unattractive companion (Geiselman *et al.* 1984). We may also assume (probably with good reason) that an attractive person is influential and this could, in turn, be advantageous to us.
- When meeting new people we pay more attention to physically attractive individuals, especially if they are women (Maner *et al.* 2003).
- Evolutionary theorists believe that physical attractiveness may be an important clue to good health and reproductive success, i.e. 'good genes', therefore they are sought as mating partners (Langlois *et al.* 2000). See Chapter 4.
- The most obvious reason (but perhaps not the most important one) is the aesthetic pleasure derived from a beautiful face and body.

Reciprocal liking

Gouldner (1960) was one of the first to suggest that we like those people who express a liking for us. This mutual attraction, known as the *reciprocity effect*, has been demonstrated in many studies (e.g. Wilson & Henzlik 1986; Sperling & Borgaro 1995) and is one of the most robust findings in interpersonal attraction research. For example, Backman and Secord (1959) found that if participants in a discussion group were led to believe that certain group members liked them, they were likely to choose these people to form a smaller group with them in a later session.

The belief that someone likes you can operate as a self-fulfilling prophecy, transforming the belief into actual reality. Curtis and Miller

(1986) gave some participants the false impression that the people with whom they were having a discussion liked them very much. These participants more frequently expressed agreement, disclosed more personal information about themselves and had a generally more positive attitude than did participants who were not led to believe they were liked. This in turn affected the people to whom they were talking in a positive way and the belief that they liked them became a fact. Similarly, Stinson *et al*. (2009) found that people who anticipated being liked by another individual acted more warmly during their interactions with that person, which in turn increased that person's liking for them.

The reciprocal liking effect can be quite complex. The people we most like are those who initially dislike us and then change their mind and come to like us (the so-called loss–gain situation). These people are actually preferred to people who have liked us all along (Aronson & Linder 1965). The people we like least are those who like us initially but then begin to dislike us.

We are, however, not completely indiscriminate when people express or indicate a liking for us. Sigall and Aronson (1969) found that male participants who were led to believe that a group of women liked them only reciprocated these feelings when the women were physically attractive, not when they were unattractive. Berscheid and Walster (1969) point out that if someone who likes us tells us things about ourselves that do not correspond to our self-concept, we will not return their liking. In addition, we are not attracted to those we belief are insincere in their expressed liking (Jones 1964).

Why is reciprocal liking important?

Basically, we like to be liked and would not find it rewarding to form a relationship with anyone who has a negative opinion of us. Being liked bolsters our self-esteem and thereby makes us feel valued.

Competence

On the whole, we prefer people who are socially skilled, intelligent and competent over those who are not. Although good looks may be the magnet that attracts us in the first place, once a relationship is underway, intelligence may be more important. Indeed, if someone is intelligent they may be assessed as being physically attractive due to the halo effect. The stereotype that 'what is beautiful is good' is turned on its head: that what is good is perceived as beautiful.

The particular area of competence that any particular individual finds attractive will depend on the nature of the relationship. Some people are attractive because they are insightful, others because they are good conversationalists and so on.

Just as positive characteristics such as competence are associated with liking, so negative characteristics are associated with dislike. One particular area of incompetence we have little time for is people who are boring. Leary et al. (1986) found that interesting participants were rated as more popular, friendly, enthusiastic and less impersonal than boring speakers.

As with the other factors, there are exception to the competence-attraction principle. Hagen and Kahn (1975) discovered that although men expressed a preference for a competent woman over an incompetent one when shown a hypothetical profile of her, in reality it was quite another story. Presented with actual women, men no longer preferred the competent one. This study highlights the constant problem of the ecological validity of studies: what is found from materials such as questionnaires does not always reflect real-life attitudes and opinions.

In addition, there is such a thing as being 'too perfect'. Most of us can appreciate that, much as we may like accomplished individuals, if they have no weak spots or flaws at all we become exasperated and irritated by them. Aronson and Worchel (1966) arranged a scenario in which an exceptionally talented individual made a minor blunder by spilling coffee. This greatly improved his popularity, probably because he suddenly became 'human' – the so-called 'pratfall effect'. However when a fairly incompetent individual did the same, the poor unfortunate became even less popular!

Why is competence important?

In general, socially skilled, competent, intelligent people are rewarding to be with whatever their particular area of competence.

Is it all just a matter of luck?

Now that we have considered all the factors that influence the formation of relationships, let us reflect on the extent to which friendship, rather than being an intentional choice based on common values and interests, is, in fact, largely a matter of chance. The work on proximity particularly emphasises the chance nature of encounters that eventually lead to the formation of long-lasting, deep friendships (Back et al. 2008). Social psychology has a rich tradition of emphasising the importance of situational factors and the work on the formation of relationships is no exception. Sir Peter Ustinov (1979), quoted by Back et al. (2008), stated that 'contrary to general belief, I do not believe that friends are necessarily the people you like best, they are merely the people who got there first' (p. 93).

Summary

The main factors that influence the formation of a relationship are:

- *Proximity*: how far a person lives or works from you. The reasons why it is influential include the fact that we prefer familiar people, there is little effort (cost) in interacting with them, we like our environment to be predicable and we expect to see them again so we might as well be friendly!
- *Similarity*: people tend to make friends with people of the same age, ethnicity, socioeconomic class, educational attainment, physical attractiveness and sex, with whom they share common interests and values. People also tend to marry people who are similar to themselves. The matching hypothesis states that, in romantic relationships, people tend to pair with those who are of a similar level of attractiveness. It is a myth that opposites attract. Complementarity only applies in terms of dominance and submission.
- *Physical attraction*: the most popular people are those who are the most physically attractive. Beautiful people are assumed to have other positive characteristics such as a kind and caring personality, intelligence and high self-esteem.
- *Reciprocal liking*: we like those who like us. Being liked boosts our self-esteem and makes us feel valued.
- *Competence*: we like people who are socially skilled, intelligent and competent.

FURTHER READING

Regan, P. (2011). *Close Relationships* (Chapter 4). New York: Routledge.

Theories of attraction

4

What this chapter will teach you

- How relationships can be explained in terms of economics – how we weigh up the gains/losses and profits of relationships. Two related theories, that of social exchange and equity, are explained.

- How evolutionary theorists explain what men and women look for when choosing a mate and parent for their offspring.

Having considered how certain factors, in particular proximity, similarity and physical attractiveness, are important in the formation of friendship and romantic relationships we now explore some of the theories that seek to explain why these and other factors may be of importance in the formation, maintenance and, on occasion, the dissolution of such relationships.

Social exchange theories

When you are in a relationship you like to think that you are 'getting something out of it' – that it's not simply take, take, take and no give.

KEY TERMS

Social exchange This theory states that people weigh up costs and benefits and behave in such a way as to maximise benefits and minimise costs. It follows that the most satisfying relationships are those with the greatest rewards at the lowest costs.

Social exchange is an economic model of human behaviour with a very simple fundamental premise, that we like to maximise benefits and minimise costs. It is economic insofar as it proposes that relationships are based on the exchange of rewards and costs between the people concerned and that the most satisfying and long-lasting relationships are those that involve the greatest rewards at the lowest cost. It applies to all kinds of relationships: those with your boss, teacher, friend or lover.

Over the years, the basic ideas of social exchange have been modified and extended such that there are various versions of the theory as applied to relationships (Homans 1961; Walster *et al*. 1978; Hatfield *et al*. 1979). The most straightforward way to view it is to look at three major factors that influence the satisfaction of a relationship: *profits*, *alternatives* and *investments*.

Profits

Homans (1961) proposed that before embarking on a relationship, we weigh up the past, present and possible future rewards and costs, and if we judge it to be profitable, the relationship will go ahead. If, on the other hand, we assess that a loss may be incurred, the relationship is likely to be a non-starter. This principle applies to both parties, so the relationship has to be mutually beneficial in order to form and survive.

As in economics, a profit or loss is calculated by rewards minus costs. Homans (1961) defined rewards very generally, as anything a person feels is valuable, so rewards may include compliments, entertaining company and material gifts. Foa and Foa (1974) identify six basic types of rewards: love, money, status, information, goods and services. Some of these rewards have value regardless of who provides them: money, for example. Other rewards, particularly love, vary in value depending on who provides them. When we say that a relationship is valuable to us, we often mean that it provides unique rewards that cannot, by definition, be obtained elsewhere. Costs can also take almost any form since they are anything that someone considers to be unpleasant, such as arguments, irritating habits or feeling obliged to cook a meal every night. The costs can come from outside: if others disapprove of the relationship and criticise us for being in it, this is a negative consequence. Naturally, different rewards and costs are important in different relationships. At work salary and productivity are likely to be determinants of relationship satisfaction whereas in intimate relationships it is love and commitment that are essential constituents of relationship stability.

Sedikides *et al.* (1994) ascertained the rewards and costs of romantic relationships among students. Rewards included companionship, sexual gratification, feeling loved, happiness, intimacy, self-understanding and social support from the partner's friends and relatives. Costs included arguments, restricted freedom to socialise, monetary losses, worry and stress about the relationship, and the time and effort necessary to devote to it. There were sex differences in these costs. More men than women mentioned cited loss of freedom to socialise and date and monetary losses. More women than men mentioned loss of identity and increased dependence on the partner.

Research evidence supports the idea that in intimate relationships, greater rewards are associated with longer endurance. Dating couples who start out having many rewarding interactions are less likely to break up than those who start with fewer rewards (Lloyd *et al.* 1984).

According to Rusbult (1983), who has analysed costs and rewards in intimate relationships, the picture for costs is not quite so straightforward. During the 'honeymoon' period of such a relationship, costs don't really come into play: for about the first three months, they tend to be ignored and therefore do not affect the degree of satisfaction with the relationship. Only later are increasing costs related to decreased satisfaction. As the theory would predict, in long-standing, cohabiting relationships, whether gay, lesbian or heterosexual, high rewards and low costs are associated with the greatest fulfilment.

Alternatives

Thibaut and Kelley (1959), in their *interdependence theory*, suggest that when we calculate whether or not a relationship is profitable and therefore satisfactory, we base it not only on the actual rewards and costs but also on comparisons with other rewards and costs. We use two dimensions by which we make these assessments: comparison level and comparison level for alternatives.

The **comparison level** is the amount of rewards we think we deserve from the relationship based on standards derived from social norms and personal expectations. Our comparison level, therefore, depends on our past experiences in relationships

> **KEY TERM**
>
> **The comparison level** The amount of rewards we think we deserve from the relationship based on standards derived from social norms and personal expectations.

and what we've come to expect based on what we see in other relationships, including those in books and films. Because we are constantly experiencing new relationships, our comparison level is liable to change over time. We may not understand why Sue seems content with her husband who does not get home until ten every night, having gone to the pub after work. But this becomes more understandable when we know that Sue was previously married to a man who was violent and did not want children, whereas in her present marriage her husband has been enthusiastic about being a father and is a good material provider. Similarly with other relationships, we are more likely to be content with a strict but fair boss if we have previously had to tolerate a bad-tempered, unfair superior rather than an easy-going, tolerant one.

The comparison level of any one person is closely related to their self-esteem. People with high self-esteem have a relatively high comparison level for interpersonal relationships – they expect to have relationships that provide a high profit level. In contrast, people with low self-esteem and therefore a low comparison level settle for relationships that show little profit or even a loss, because this is all they expect and/or believe they deserve.

The **comparison level for alternatives** is the amount of costs and rewards we believe are available from alternative relationships. Thibaut and Kelley recognised that we cannot consider rewards and costs in isolation but must take account of the context of what else is available.

KEY TERM

The comparison level for alternatives The amount of costs and rewards we believe are available from alternative relationships.

All relationships, but especially sexual ones, entail limitations being put on other relationships. If we spend lots of time with one group of friends, it inevitably limits the time available for others, and if we are in an intimate relationship, the usual (but not invariable) expectation is that we no longer have sexual relationships with other people. Chris might be quite content in a relationship that is comfortable but has never been desperately romantic until he is 'swept off his feet' by a new work colleague. It has been suggested that some people remain in very unsatisfactory relationships because they believe that the alternative of being alone is worse.

Just as the amount of commitment we make to a relationship depends to some extent on the alternatives, so the commitment influences the way we perceive the alternatives. When developing a relationship, individuals gradually close themselves off from attractive alternatives. Simpson (1990) found that people who were dating someone viewed members of the opposite sex as less attractive than did those who were not courting. Johnson and Rusbult (1989) arranged for highly committed individuals to interact with an attractive member of the opposite sex on a computer dating exercise. They found that these individuals were particularly derogatory about these potential threats to their relationship. Duck (1994) argued that the state of a current relationship helps determine how attractive the alternatives appear. He points out that there are always alternative partners in an objective sense but we only notice them when we are fed up with what we have. Those who are committed are less interested in alternatives and see them as relatively unattractive. Despite this, it should be noted that an attractive person is still one of the major contributors to the breakup of a relationship (Buunk, 1987).

Investments

Rusbult (1983) adds a further element to social exchange theory by suggesting that commitment to a relationship does not only depend on outcomes and available alternatives but on the *amount of investment* that has been made. Once a well-established relationship begins to pall we can pack our things, collect the cat and go – but it's not that easy. We have put time, effort and money into the relationship. We share possessions and mutual friends. We may have given up career opportunities and other romantic alternatives. We may also feel that we have given our partner the 'best years of our life' and now have less to offer someone else. According to Rusbult, the greater the investment, the greater the commitment, and the more likely we are to stay. Investments, then, not only increase commitment but also serve to stabilise a relationship.

We have already noted several research studies that lend support to this model. In addition, other studies have shown that it does effectively predict how long a premarital relationship will last (Cate & Lloyd 1992) and helps to account for why people return to an abusive relationship (Rusbult & Martz 1995). Nevertheless, despite this support, there are some limitations and criticisms of this approach.

First, most of the research has been conducted on short-term relationships with student samples and little on married relationships over a wider population.

Second, this model says very little about individual differences in people's willingness to commit to a relationship. Commitment may be more

> **REFLECTIVE EXERCISE 4.1**
>
> Much has been written about the reasons why women (and occasionally men) return to abusive relationships. One extremely controversial idea is that they some women are 'drawn' to abusive men and do not really want to escape. Social exchange theory gives a very different interpretation. Have a look at the following articles and consider this for yourself:
>
> Lerner, C. & Thomas, L. (2000) Stay-leave decision making in battered women: Trauma, coping and self-efficacy. *Cognitive Therapy and Research, 24,* 215–232.
> Pape, K. & Arias, I. (2000) The role of perceptions and attributions in battered women's intentions to permanently end their violent relationships. *Cognitive Therapy and Research, 24,* 201–214.
> Rusbult, C.E. & Martz, J.M. (1995) Remaining in an abusive relationship: An investment model analysis of non-voluntary dependence. *Personality and Social Psychology Bulletin, 21,* 558–571.

dependent on a person's willingness to trust another based on earlier experiences than on the rewards and investments (recall what was discussed in Chapter 1 about the effect of early attachment on adult relationships).

Third, valid theories should have predictability and this is not always the case with the social exchange approach. When considering the comparison level for alternatives, Pennington (1986) pointed out that social exchange theories do not predict the level at which a relationship has become so unsatisfactory that a person will leave, despite having no other relationship to turn to. Pennington suggests that the approach needs to include a notion of general expectation that specifies the minimum that people expect from a relationship. In other words, it ought to specify the level of satisfaction below which a person would leave even if there were no new relationship.

Fourth, and probably the most fundamental criticism, is the idea that in many relationships, but especially in long-term sexual ones, people do not behave like level-headed accountants motivated only by maximising their profits. Where in this approach are the ecstasies and agonies of falling in and out of love? Intimate relationships, especially at the beginning and end, are characterised by intense emotions and extravagant and impulsive actions that have no mention here. As Berscheid (1983) pointed out, attraction as a mental calculation has received considerable attention; attraction as raw emotion has received considerably less.

Nevertheless, this approach does offer a plausible account for much of the time spent in a romantic relationship as well as for the course of other relationships, such as those with friends, work colleagues and neighbours. Ultimately, though, some psychologists reject outright the notion implicit in this approach that true altruism plays no part in human relationships. They do not believe that relationships never involve freely and lovingly giving yourself to someone else in the absence of reward (e.g. Rubin 1973; Clark & Mills 1979).

Equity theory

Equity theory, formulated by Walster *et al.* (1978), is a specific version of how social exchange operates in interpersonal relationships and is derived from Homans' (1961) original social exchange theory. The equity principle states that people will only consider a relationship to be 'fair' and satisfactory if what they gain from a relationship reflects what they put in. Equity is not the same as equality. If one partner puts more into the relationship, they should get more out of it. If this is not the case, they feel exploited or that they are taking unfair advantage of their partner.

Hatfield *et al.* (1985) devised the Hatfield Global Measure in order to assess levels of equity. Research participants were asked 'Considering what you put into your dating relationship or marriage, compared to what you get out of it … and what your partner puts in compared to what (s)he gets out of it, how does your dating relationship or marriage "stack up"?' Respondents were given graded response options varying from 'I am getting a much better deal than my partner' (score +3) through 'We are getting an equally good, or bad, deal' (score 0) to 'My partner is getting a much better deal than I am' (score −3) (examples provided in Hatfield *et al.* 2008). On the basis of their answers people can be classified as over-benefitted, equitably treated or under-benefitted.

Equity theory predicts that a relationship in which a partner is over-benefitted or under-benefitted will not be a happy one. Because the imbalance generates psychological distress, which erodes the relationship, under-benefitted individuals tend to feel angry, resentful and deprived. Those who are over-benefited may feel shame, guilt and discomfort. Although both imbalances are unhappy states, it is not surprising that being under-benefitted leads to greater dissatisfaction than being over-benefitted (Hatfield *et al.* 1982). People prefer to receive too much rather than too little, even if it makes them feel uneasy.

Men and women appear to have different attitudes and responses to inequity. Hatfield *et al.* (1985) found that women are more distressed about being over-benefitted whereas men are more distressed about being under-benefitted. This may reflect other research evidence indicating that in general men care more about rewards, whereas women are more concerned for the welfare of others, especially those in their care. Prins *et al.* (1992) found that women but not men in inequitable relationships are likely to engage in extramarital affairs, presumably in order to give what they perceive to be a more equitable balance to the relationship.

There are individual differences in the extent to which equity matters in close relationships. Buunk and Van Yperen (1991) used the Hatfield Global Measure to assess equity and also measured satisfaction on an 8-item Likert scale that measured the frequency with which an interaction with the partner in an intimate relationship was seen as rewarding and as aversive. They found individual differences in the degree to which people were concerned about equity: those they referred to as high in exchange orientation were dissatisfied by being over-benefitted or under-benefitted but those low in exchange orientation were far less affected by inequity. In addition, those low in exchange orientation were far more satisfied within their relationship than those high in exchange orientation. This can be viewed as a criticism of equity theory, since people low in exchange orientation don't appear to mind about equity.

RESEARCH ISSUE AND DISCUSS AND DEBATE

You can view the Hatfield Global Measure (of equity) and other similar measures at:
www.elainehatfield.com/equity.doc.

You may wish to use it to do some of your own research. This website also references measures of reliability and validity – useful for evaluating the methodology of the research.

Equally interesting, have a look at all the different measures that are used to assess equity (e.g. personal concerns, emotional concerns, day-to-day concerns, opportunities gained and lost) and see whether or not you, personally, think they are important and a good way of assessing the equity of a relationship.

Is the concept of equity universal or do cultures differ in the extent to which it is valued? In order to investigate its cultural robustness, Aumer-Ryan *et al.* (2006) interviewed large samples of Japanese-American, West Indian and multicultural internet users and found that in all cultures people considered equity to be of great importance in marriage and courting relationships. Nevertheless, the researchers did find important cultural differences in equity. Aumer-Ryan *et al.* (2007) interviewed men and women from the University of Hawaii, a relatively individualistic culture and people from a University in Jamaica, considered a more collectivist culture. They again found that in both cultures equity was considered to be of critical importance in romantic relationships but there was a difference between them. In Hawaii people considered their relationships to be slightly more equitable and far more satisfying than did people in Jamaica. The latter were most satisfied when they over-benefitted from a relationship whereas the people from Hawaii were most satisfied when their relationship was equitable. The researchers concluded that equity was less important in collectivist Jamaica than in individualistic Hawaii.

As with social exchange, there is a considerable body of research evidence that supports equity theory. There is abundant evidence that the more socially desirable a person is, i.e. the more physically attractive, rich and famous they are, the more likely they are to have a socially desirable partner. We saw earlier that couples tend to be matched in terms of physical health, looks, intelligence, education and self-esteem. Dating couples are more likely to commit if their relationship is seen as equitable. Walster *et al.* (1978) asked over 500 college men and women involved in romantic relationships to judge how equitable this relationship was. As predicted by the theory, after three months, students in inequitable relationships were more likely to have ended them. Traupmann et al. (1983) found that men and women who felt their relationship was equitable were far more content with them than those who felt their relationship was inequitable. Equity has been found to relate to many aspects of relationships, and appears to be important throughout a couple's lifetime (Pillemer et al. 2008).

Additional supporting evidence comes from the fact that people in inequitable relationships are more likely to engage in extramarital affairs than their peers and that equitable relationships are more likely to endure and be satisfactory than inequitable ones.

Market considerations, i.e. considerations of the social desirability of a potential partner, have been found to affect gay, lesbian and heterosexual relationships as demonstrated by the fact that in all of these relationships attractive individuals are more prized than unattractive ones (e.g. Buunk & Van Yperen 1989; Van Yperen & Buunk 1990). Equity has been shown to be important in sparking passionate love, sexual attraction and in promoting satisfaction and stability in long-term intimate relationships (e.g. Byers & Wang 2004).

Generally theorists have no problem with applying equity theory to non-intimate relationships such as acquaintances, employer/employee and customer/proprietor, but there is considerable controversy over whether the principles of equity apply to intimate relationships. One group of psychologists believes that this principle applies to all relationships, pointing to the plentiful research that backs up the argument that inequity leads to dissatisfaction (e.g. Buunk & Van Yperen 1991; DeMaris & Longmore 1996; Frisco & Williams 2003). Some equally prominent psychologists maintain that people are not primarily concerned with reward and fairness in their love relationships and that unconditional love does exist. Prominent among these is Clark (1986) who distinguishes between two types of relationship: communal relationships and exchange relationships. In exchange relationships, such as those at work or with acquaintances, there is no special responsibility for the other person's welfare and equity is the basis on which such relationships operate. In communal relationships, such as family relationships and marriage, in which another's welfare is paramount, very different norms prevail. Men and women wish to please their partners, children or other close relatives, to care for them and nurture them and are not concerned with 'keeping score'. According to Clark and others, very close relationships involve a commitment that is selfless and transcends economic considerations. This is backed by research that finds little evidence that inequity is important in intimate relationships (e.g. Felmlee et al. 1990; Gager & Sanchez 2003). Indeed, research conducted by Clark and Mills (1979) indicates that people in the early stages of a relationship interpret the need to reciprocate as a sign that the other person is not interested in a romantic liaison. Hatfield *et al.* (2008) have countered this criticism by pointing to the fact that even in Clark's research, people who made sacrifices on behalf of their partners did expect gratitude and reciprocation should the need arise (Grote & Clark 2004).

There are other criticisms of equity theory. Cate and Lloyd (1988) believe that it is the absolute level of rewards rather than fairness that predicts the satisfaction in love relationships. In general, the more we receive good things from a relationship, the better we feel about it. Rewards such as love, status and sexual satisfaction are more important to us than perfect equity in the exchange of rewards.

Evolutionary theory

We now turn from economics to evolution for an explanation of who chooses whom in relationships. Unlike the previous theories, this one does not seek to explain the choices we make in all relationships, but what people seek in heterosexual attachments.

Sociobiology applies the principles of evolution to the understanding of social behaviour. The theory argues that the behaviour of all animals has evolved so that it maximises the likelihood that individuals will pass on their genes to future generations. In human terms, this means that both women and men unconsciously behave in ways that promote conception, birth and survival of their offspring. They will seek partners who are physically attractive since this is an important indicator of good health and reproductive fitness. Evolutionary theorists argue that standards of beauty are biological not cultural; that although there are some cultural, personal and individual differences in what is considered attractive, there is little evidence to support the idea that 'beauty is in the eye of the beholder'. This is supported by the fact that people in different cultures generally agree on which faces are attractive (Cunningham *et al.* 1995; Langlois *et al.* 2000) and greatly prefer them to unattractive faces. This preference starts early in life, before cultural standards of beauty are likely to have been assimilated (Rubenstein *et al.* 1999). Rhodes (2006) suggests that the characteristics that make a face attractive are averageness, symmetry and sexual dimorphism (for feminine traits in female faces and masculine traits in male faces). She points out that these characteristics may signal good mate quality, i.e. good health. Attractive mates (i.e. healthy ones) would provide direct benefits, such as reduced risk of contagion, caretaking abilities and/or indirect genetic benefits such as heritable resistance to disease (see Møller & Alatalo 1999). It follows from this that preference for attractive traits increases the viability of offspring.

Rhodes (2006) has found some limited support for the association between facial attractiveness and good health but also admits to some limitations. In nonclinical samples, links with health have been found for averageness and masculinity (male faces) but not for symmetry or femininity (female faces). Research on the evolutionary psychology of facial attraction has some way yet to go.

A further important aspect of evolutionary theory is the contention that, whereas both sexes are similar in the pursuit of attractive partners, the optimal mating behaviour differs dramatically between men and women. In his *parental investment theory*, Trivers (1972) points out that men and women make very different contributions to parenting and this means that men and women will use very different criteria by which to choose their mates. Since a man can, in theory, impregnate many women within a short time and will only waste some easily replaceable sperm if sexual intercourse does not result in preg-

nancy, it is in his interest to be promiscuous and seek out good child-bearers. A woman, who has to invest a great deal more in bearing each child than does a man, is likely to be far more choosy when selecting a mate. She will be coy, take her time and choose a man who can provide for her and her infant – perhaps an older man who is established in his career. As Davis (1990) succinctly put it, in search for a heterosexual partner we view 'men as success objects, women as sex objects'.

Some research does support the fact that men tend to give a high priority to youth and beauty (which are taken as indicators of child-bearing potential) while women prefer older men of higher educational and occupational status (indicative of the ability to support the children and partner). For example, men are attracted to women with a low waist-to-hip ratio (WHR) and this is related to child-bearing potential (Singh 1993). Buss (1989), in an extensive study of thirty-seven cultures (in thirty-three countries), analysed the results of more than 10,000 questionnaires asking respondents to rate a number of factors such as age, intelligence and

Figure 4.1 'Is that a real wad in your pocket or just a flexible friend?' (Cartoon by Roy Hunt).

sociability, for their importance in a sexual partner. Consistent with sociobiological theory, findings were that men valued physical attractiveness more than did women, while women were more likely than men to value good earning potential and high occupational status. In all the cultures, both women and men preferred the man to be the older of the pair. Further support comes from research that demonstrates that people are especially attentive to high status men (but not women) and to physically attractive women (Maner *et al.* 2003, 2008).

A further aspect of this theory is concerned with the nature of jealousy. For humans an enduring pair-bond increases the survival chances of the individuals and their offspring (Fortunato & Archetti 2010); jealousy serves to protect the relationship because the emotion leads an individual to behave in a way that shields the partner from the rival. Sociobiology predicts that there will be sex differences in the type of rival a person feels jealous towards: females should be jealous of attractive other women whilst males should be jealous of rivals of higher status.

In support of these contentions, Dijkstra and Buunk (2002) have found these predicted sex differences in rival characteristics that evoke jealousy in heterosexuals. Massar and Buunk (2010) have demonstrated that women subliminally exposed to an attractive woman reported significantly more jealousy than women exposed to an unattractive rival in a scenario read to them. Buunk and Dijkstra (2001) have also found predicted differences between males and females in homosexual samples. They concluded that males and females possess an 'evolved sex-specific rival-orientated mechanism through which they respond more or less automatically to those rival characteristics that have been important in sexual selection in our evolutionary past' (p. 391).

The evolutionary approach also offers an explanation for the intense emotions involved in falling in love. Kenrick and Trost (1989) believe that passionate love has evolved as an innate behaviour to ensure strong pair bonding and thereby a secure family unit in which to nurture the young. Attachment bonds between parents greatly enhance the survival of their offspring (Zeifman & Hazan 2000). Love, therefore, is seen as an evolutionary device to keep couples together long enough to nurture their offspring. This may offer a more plausible account of romantic love and the intensity of the emotion involved than does the exchange model of level-headed calculation of assets.

However, this approach is not without its detractors. Despite the contention that there are universal standards of beauty, some studies indicate that there are significant historical and cultural differences in heterosexual mate selection. For example, men's preference for younger women was considerably greater in the past than it is now and is greater in traditional than in modern societies (Glenn 1989). The contention that a WHR of 0.7 is universally attractive has been questioned by Marlowe and Wetsman. They criticise the findings of Singh (1993; and also Singh & Luis 1995; Furnham *et al.* 1997) because these preferences were only tested on college students. These researchers found that in foraging societies, in which there is no risk of obesity, there is a preference for women with higher WHR (Wetsman & Marlowe 1999; Marlowe & Wetsman 2001). In order to understand what drives preferences we need to look at a whole range of cultures including a variety of subsistence-orientated ones and so far this has not been done. There is also evidence that WHR is less important than Body Mass Index (BMI) in judgements of attractiveness (Streeter & McBurney 2003; Tovée *et al.* 2003; Smith *et al.* 2007a). Swami and Tovée (2012) found that men under stress prefer heavier female body sizes. This implies that judgements of attractiveness vary depending on local ecologies and adapt according to environmental conditions. This does not necessarily contradict the evolutionary approach since men may have evolved strategies to help them best cope with local environmental conditions but it does imply that simple measures of preference for a particular BMI or WHR provide questionable support for it.

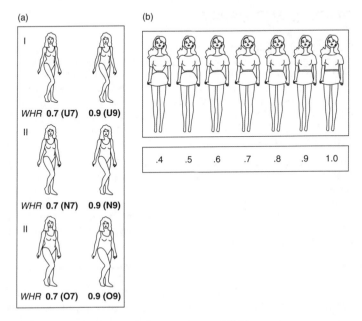

Figure 4.2 Hip to waist ratios (from Marlowe & Wetsman 2001).

Some researchers also question the basic assumption of evolutionary theory that certain physical characteristics (such as a certain WHR or facial symmetry) are honest signals of health and therefore of reproductive potential. Smith *et al*. (2007b) found that cardiovascular fitness, which is related to health, was only a very weak cue to judging attractiveness, calling into question the assumption that health plays a role in attractiveness judgements.

In addition, some psychologists argue that mate preferences may, to some extent, depend on the type of relationship that is sought: for example, both men and women put relatively more emphasis on physical attractiveness in short-term sexual relationships than in long-term relationships (Li & Kenrick 2006; Maner *et al*. 2008). Gustavsson *et al*. (2008), looking at personal advertisements in a Swedish newspaper, found limited support for the gender differences in mate selection. Females did, as predicted, ask for resources more often than did males but there were no sex differences in the proportion of those either offering attractiveness or seeking it. These researchers point to evidence that suggests that females in more egalitarian situations tend to put relatively more emphasis on attractiveness than on resources in a mate in short-term relationships, implying that social factors do influence mate selection (Eagly & Wood 1999; Moore & Cassidy 2007).

DISCUSS AND DEBATE

Davis (1990) conducted a content analysis of personal advertisements in a Canadian newspaper and found consistent sex differences in the attributes sought by men and women. He found that physical characteristics were more often requested by men than women ('male, 40 seeks blonde, slim 21-year-old for romps in the hay') and employment attributes were more often requested by women than men ('Woman, 40 seeks professional, financially independent man with whom to invest her assets'.) [Examples not real!]

But Gustavsson *et al*.'s (2008) study, using data from a different time and country, found that, although there were predicted gender differences in requesting resources, there were no gender differences in offering and seeking attractiveness. Why do you think these results may differ? Look at one or two of the dating websites or in your local newspapers and see if there are any sex differences in the dating attributes described and requested.

The major limitation of sociobiological explanations in general is that they observe existing behaviour patterns and then use hindsight to explain this behaviour in terms of why it has evolved. One important characteristic of a good theory is that it can be used to make predictions about the future, yet sociobiology has little predictive value. There are so many possibilities with regard to how behaviour may evolve that prediction becomes impossible.

The difficulty of separating culture from evolution will always mean that sociobiology is likely to remain controversial. Nevertheless, although evolutionary explanations of mate preference remain speculative and controversial, they do serve to remind us that sexual relationships fulfil an important biological function and satisfy such a basic need that evolution has doubtless had an influence on our behaviour in this area. Ascertaining the exact extent and shape of that influence requires a good deal of further research.

Summary

- Social exchange theory (SET) states that within relationships we seek to maximise rewards and minimise costs. In order to do this, we consider:
  - The profits (rewards less costs).
  - The alternatives: Thibaut and Kelley (1959) interdependence theory. We take account of the comparison level (the rewards we think we deserve) and comparison level for alternatives (the rewards/costs offered by other incompatible relationships).
  - The investments already made in the relationship (e.g. time, effort, money, sacrifices).
- Equity theory (Walster *et al.* 1978) states that people will only consider a relationship to be fair if what they gain from it reflects what they put in. If they put in more than they get out then they are under-benefitted; if they get more out than they put in they are over-benefitted; both situations are unsatisfactory. Although equity is important in most relationships, there are individual differences and cultural variations in the degree to which it influences satisfaction.
- Some psychologists believe that market forces (as put forward by SET and equity theory) have no part in love relationships and that unconditional love does exist. Clark (1986) argues that some relationships, such as with family and lovers, are 'communal'. They transcend economic considerations and are selfless, concerned only with the welfare of others.

- Evolutionary theory argues that behaviour in relationships is unconsciously controlled by ways that promote the survival of genes into subsequent generations. Men are inclined towards promiscuity as this increases opportunities for producing offspring. In contrast, women, who invest far more biologically in producing offspring and are very limited in how many they can produce, are inclined towards selectivity and coyness in their choice of mate in order to ensure the best father for their offspring. In line with this, men are preoccupied with youth and beauty in their choice of sexual partner while women are concerned with status and financial stability.
- Parental investment theory (Trivers 1972) argues that women make a much greater (biological) investment in parenting than do men. This results in men and women using very different criteria for choosing a mate. Men desire attractive, youthful women since this implies good child-bearing potential; women desire men who are successful and financially secure who can provide for her and her offspring.

FURTHER READING

Buss, D.M. (1989) Sex differences in human mate preferences: Evolutionary hypotheses tested in 37 cultures. *Behavioral and Brain Sciences*, *12*, 1–14.

Buss, D.M. (2000) *The Dangerous Passion: Why Jealousy Is as Necessary as Love and Sex*. New York: Free Press.

Simpson, J.A. & Rholes, W.S. (Eds.) (1998) *Attachment Theory and Close Relationships* (Chapter 13). New York: Guilford Press.

Types of love

5

What this chapter will teach you

- The distinction between liking and loving.
- The distinction between companionate and passionate love.
- How liking and loving can be measured.
- Theories of love, including Sternberg's triangular theory and Lee's 'colours of love' typology.
- How adult styles of loving may be related to early experiences of attachment.

Liking and loving

We start this chapter with an apt quotation (used by Hatfield *et al.* 1986), from Liebowitz (1983, pp. 48–49):

> Love is, by definition, the strongest positive feeling we can have. … Other things – stimulant drugs, passionate causes, manic states – can induce powerful changes in our brains, but none so reliably, so enduringly, or so delightfully as the 'right' person. … If the relationship is not established or is uncertain, anxiety or other displeasure

centers may be quite active as well, producing a situation of great emotional turmoil as the lover swings between hope and torment.

Although we use the expression 'love' to describe our feelings towards our closest friends, our parents and our romantic partners, we know that the emotions we feel in each case are by no means identical. We also appreciate that when we talk of *liking* one particular friend and *loving* another, the feelings we have for each of them may not be so very different. They vary in quantity rather than in quality. We will take a look at the way social psychologists classify different types of love.

Berscheid and Walster (1978) distingish between *liking*, *companionate love* and *passionate (romantic) love*. Liking and **companionate love** are considered to be extremes on a continuum, the only difference being the depth of feeling and the degree of involvement. It is the love we feel for friends and family. **Passionate love**, on the other hand, is quite a different matter. It has been defined as:

KEY TERMS

Companionate love The affection we feel for those with whom our lives are deeply entwined.

Passionate love A powerful emotional state that involves feelings of tenderness, elation, anxiety and sexual desire.

A state of intense longing for union with another. Passionate love is a complex functional whole including appraisals or appreciations, subjective feelings, expressions, patterned physiological processes, action tendencies, and instrumental behaviors. Reciprocated love (union with another) is associated with fulfilment and ecstasy. Unrequited love (separation) with emptiness, anxiety, or despair.

(Hatfield & Rapson, 1993, p. 5)

In essence:

- *Liking* is the affection we feel for casual acquaintances.
- *Companionate love* is the affection we feel for those with whom our lives are deeply entwined.
- *Passionate love* is a powerful emotional state that involves overwhelming feelings of tenderness, elation, anxiety and sexual desire.

Berscheid *et al.* (1989) and Hatfield and Walster (1978) suggest that the important differences between companionate and passionate love are:

- Companionate love (and liking) develops through mutual actual rewards while passionate love is based on imagined gratification and fantasy.

- Passionate love becomes diluted over time whereas companionate love tends to deepen and intensify.
- Passionate love thrives on novelty and uncertainty while companionate love is founded on familiarity and predictability.
- Companionate love is a totally positive emotion, whereas the emotions involved in passionate love are both positive and negative. When we fall in love, we experience joy and excitement, jealousy and anxiety.

Rubin's model of liking and loving

In order to explore the concepts of liking and different types of loving, it is necessary to have some means of measuring them. Rubin (1970, 1973), one of the first social psychologists to attempt to measure liking and love, devised both a Love scale and a Liking scale. The research carried out to compile these scales also led Rubin to draw a distinction between liking and the type of loving as expressed by dating couples. The *Liking scale* contains two characteristics:

- Similarity to oneself.
- Respect for the other person.

The *Love Scale* consists of three components:

- *Attachment:* A strong need for the physical presence and support of the loved one and the desire to be fulfilled by them.
- *Caring:* A feeling of concern for the loved one manifested in the desire to help and support them.
- *Intimacy:* A desire for close and confidential contact with the loved one in an atmosphere of trust.

Rubin asked dating couples to complete both the Liking and Loving scales as applied to their dating partner and to a close friend. Here are some items from both scales: the first three are from the Liking scale and the last three from the Loving scale (based on Rubin 1973). For each item, the answer is on a scale from 1 = *not at all* to 10 = *totally*.

1   This person is one of the most likeable people I know.
2   This person is the sort of person I would like to be.
3   I have great confidence in this person's good judgements.
4   I feel I can confide in this person about virtually anything.
5   I would forgive this person for practically anything.
6   I would do almost anything for this person.

Rubin found that with regard to how the couples felt about each other there was not much difference between the men and women in the love they expressed, but the women tended to like the men more than the men liked the women! Men and women rated liking for same-sex friends equally, but women tended to express more love for their friends. It has been suggested that with regard to adult relationships, men tend to love only within the context of a sexual relationship whereas women are more likely to experience at least some of the components of attachment, caring and, to a lesser extent, intimacy with a wide variety of people.

Although some have argued that it is impossible to measure love, results show that the scales devised by Rubin do have some validity. In experimental sessions, Rubin (1973) found that couples who scored high on the Love scale made more eye contact and were more likely to say they were in love. In a six-month follow-up study, scores on the Rubin Love scale successfully predicted how successful a relationship was. People who scored high on the Love scale were more likely to be still together and to have committed themselves to a permanent relationship.

We will now turn to other ways in which types of love have been classified. You will notice that though these classifications are more complex than that of the simple differentiation between passionate and companionate love, they all use this as a basic distinction.

Sternberg's Triangle of Love

Sternberg (1986) presented a triangular theory of love, which deals with both the nature of love itself and with loves in different kinds of relationships. He sees love as having three central components:

- Intimacy – the *emotional* component. This involves sharing, mutual understanding and emotional support. It creates warmth, closeness and a feeling of bondedness in a relationship.
- Passion – the *motivational* component. This involves physical attraction, sexual desire and consummation, the feeling of being 'in love' and an intense desire for union with the other. Although sexual needs are very important in passion, other needs may also be involved, such as the need for self-esteem, nurturance, affiliation, succour, dominance and submission.
- Commitment/decision – the *cognitive* component. This involves a short-term decision that you love someone and a longer-term commitment to maintain that love. These two aspects do not necessarily go together: a person can love another without being

committed to love in the longer term; conversely, a person can be committed to a relationship without acknowledging any love for the other person.

According to Sternberg, the *amount* of love we experience depends on the absolute strength of the three components, and the *kind* of love we experience depends on their strengths relative to each other. The components interact with each other and with the actions that they produce so as to form a number of different kinds of loving experiences. Depending on whether the level of each component is high or low, there are eight possible combinations and each of these combinations produces a different type of love (or, to be precise, seven types of love and one non-love). For example, when passion is high but commitment and intimacy are low, this produces infatuation. The types of love are shown in Table 5.1.

Sternberg suggests that love can be understood in terms of these three components that together can be viewed in as forming the corners of a triangle (see Figure 5.1). The geometry of the triangle depends on two factors:

- the actual amount of love
- the balance of love (the differing amounts of each component).

Not surprisingly, relationships built on two or more elements of love are more enduring than those based on a single component. Consummate love, the only type built on all three, is the strongest and most enduring, but is rare.

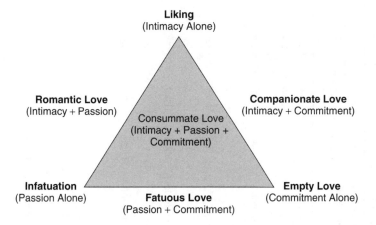

Figure 5.1 Sternberg's (1986) triangular model of love.

Table 5.1 The components of Sternberg's (1986) triangular theory of love

Type of love relationship	Component			Example
	Intimacy	Passion	Commitment/decision	
Non-love	Low	Low	Low	The feeling we have for casual acquaintances.
Liking	High	Low	Low	The feeling involved in true and deep friendships. There is closeness and warmth but no passion or long-term commitment.
Infatuation	Low	High	Low	Obsession with an idealised partner rather than a real person, typical of 'love at first sight'. It involves a high degree of physical and mental arousal and tends to last only if the relationship is not consummated.
Empty love	Low	Low	High	Typical of the kind of love in a long-term stagnant relationship in which people have lost mutual emotional involvement and stay together due to habit, fear of change or 'for the sake of the children'.
Romantic love	High	High	Low	Love based on both physical and emotional attraction. Typical of the love between Romeo and Juliet in which the lovers feel mutual passion accompanied by the feeling that they can bare their souls to one another.
Companionate love	High	Low	High	The love that exists in a long-term committed friendship or in a marriage in which physical attraction has waned. Most romantic love relationships that last eventually turn into companionate love relationships.
Fatuous love	Low	High	High	Commitment made on the basis of passion alone as typified by a 'whirlwind romance'. Because intimacy has had no time to develop, and passion soon fades, partners feel short-changed and disappointed and the relationship is likely to be very short-lived.
Consummate love	High	High	High	A complete love towards which many people strive, especially in romantic relationships. We do not seek this kind of love in many of our relationships, just those that mean the most to us.

Sternberg proposed that the components differ from each other in important ways, including:

- *Stability* – some of the components are more enduring than others. As you can probably guess, the components of intimacy and commitment are both fairly stable but passion is less predictable.
- *Conscious controllability* – we tend to assume we have conscious control over commitment but relatively little over the extent of sexual attraction (i.e. passion) we feel for a partner. Maybe we can't help being 'swept off our feet' but what we do about it is up to us.
- *Experiential salience* – This refers to the amount of conscious awareness we have of how we feel. While we tend to be aware of the amount of passion we feel, strangely, we may not fully realise the extent of our commitment (sometimes this only becomes obvious when the relationship is threatened and we suddenly realise how much our lover means to us). We may also experience closeness and warmth (the intimacy component) without ever being able to fully identify it.

> **KEY TERMS**
>
> **Infatuation** Obsession with an idealised partner.
>
> **Empty love** The kind of love in a stagnant relationship with no mutual emotional involvement.
>
> **Romantic love** Love based on both physical and emotional attraction.
>
> **Fatuous love** The type of love that is based on passion alone with no intimacy.
>
> **Consummate love** A complete love desired by many in romantic relationships.

Sternberg also suggests that each of the three components – intimacy, passion and commitment/decision – differs in how long it lasts and the speed with which it fades. Passion rises quickly and then typically fades fast; commitment gradually rises and then levels off; intimacy grows slowly and steadily over a period of time. Part of the success, or otherwise, of relationships depends on our ability to change as each of the components changes.

Sternberg's theory, unlike most of its predecessors, offers more than one or two kinds of love. It therefore helps us to see love as a multiple rather than a unitary phenomenon. It also has face validity in that it reflects our own first-hand experiences in everyday life. If the triangular theory of love is valid, then different relationships ought to show different blends of the three components and this was shown to be the case (Sternberg 1997). For example, passion was higher in lover relationships relative to other relationships.

The theory also has certain practical applications. Firstly, by measuring the three components, it is possible to get a sense of where each partner in a loving relationship stands. Secondly, by analysing differences between the types of love shown by both members of a couple, it helps pinpoint areas where change and compromise may be necessary if the relationship is to endure.

Cramer (1998) argues that one problem with the model is that the decision/commitment component is not clearly defined, and it is therefore difficult to ascertain on what basis an individual decides to love another person). If it is on the basis of intimacy and passion (the other two components) then the category of empty love disappears.

Lee's 'colours of love' typology

Using a rather innovative approach to the classification of love, Lee (1973) compared styles of loving to types of colours. Just as there are three primary colours that can then be combined to form secondary colours so, according to Lee, there are three basic styles of loving, which can then be combined in different ways to produce secondary styles of love.

The three primary styles of love are:

- **Eros** (romantic love); an all-consuming emotional experience, an immediate powerful physical attraction to someone.
- **Ludus** (game-playing love): love based on fun and strategy with no commitment and a belief in 'playing the field'. It is usually short-lived and will end as soon as boredom sets in.
- **Storge** (companionate love): A comfortable intimacy that grows slowly and involves mutual sharing and gradual self-disclosure. It was described by Lee (1973) as 'love without fever or folly'.

The three secondary styles identified by Lee are:

- **Mania**: eros + ludus (possessive/obsessive love) – an emotionally intense, jealous, obsessive love shown by an anxious individual who lives in constant fear of rejection.
- **Pragma**: storge + ludus (realistic/practical love) – a logical love based on selecting a partner who satisfies practical needs and is a match in terms of age, religion, background and personality. There is contentment rather than excitement.
- **Agape**: eros + storge (altruistic/selfless love) – an unconditional, caring, giving and forgiving type of love. There is no expectation of reciprocity; love is self-sacrificing.

Lee's theory therefore involves a total of six types of love, the secondary ones having elements of primary love styles but also having their own unique characteristics.

Figure 5.2 Agape.

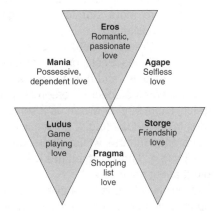

Figure 5.3 Lee's 'colours of love' wheel.

These love styles can be seen in terms of Sternberg's components. Romantic love (eros), for example, has large amounts of passion while companionate love (storge) has high degrees of commitment and intimacy but little passion.

Hendrick and Hendrick (1986, 1989) developed a self-report questionnaire called the Love Attitudes Scale (LAS) to empirically investigate these love styles with a separate scale for each of the six styles. Respondents indicate their level of agreement or disagreement with the LAS items, examples of which include 'I feel that my lover and I were meant for

KEY TERMS

Eros Romantic love.

Ludus Game-playing love.

Storge Companionate love.

Mania Possessive/obsessive love.

Pragma Realistic, practical love.

Agape Altruistic, selfless love.

each other' (Eros) and 'Our love is the best kind because it grew out of a long friendship' (Storge). Hendrick and Hendrick (1986) found good internal reliability for each scale and low intercorrelations between them, supporting the idea of distinct love styles. They also found a significant relationship between love attitudes and several background variables including gender, ethnicity, previous love experience and self-esteem.

Hendrick *et al.* (1988) found that dating couples tend to have similar love styles and that relationships based on similar love styles were more likely to endure (at least over the next few months) than those that were based on different styles. Hendrick *et al.* (1984) found strong sex differences in love styles: men were more erotic and ludic, and women were more storgic and pragmatic than the opposite sex.

Cramer (1998) criticises Hendrick's Love Attitudes Scale on the grounds that it confounds three aspects of attitudes and behaviour towards love. Some items assess attitudes towards a specific person (e.g. 'My lover and I have the right "physical chemistry" between us'); some are concerned with general attitudes towards love (e.g. 'I enjoy playing the "game of love" with several different partners); whilst others look at characteristics of past relationships (e.g. 'I have sometimes had to keep two of my lovers from finding out about each other').

Cramer (1987) administered a questionnaire based on Lee's styles of loving to a group of British undergraduates. He suggested that the items can be meaningfully grouped into four categories: relationship satisfaction, relationship openness, relationship importance and physical intimacy. The scores on these four factors correlated with five of Lee's love styles – those of romantic love (eros), possessive love (mania), companionate love (storge), pragmatic love (pragma) and game-playing love (ludus). For example, physical intimacy was positively correlated with eros but negatively correlated with storge. The factors of relationship satisfaction, relationship openness, relationship importance and physical intimacy could therefore be used to differentiate the love styles.

The theories of Lee and Sternberg are largely descriptive; they tell us which styles people use but say little about why these styles have been adopted. The next theory attempts to do just this by drawing parallels between childhood experiences and later adult relationships.

REFLECTIVE EXERCISE 5.1

You can obtain a copy of a short version of the Love Attitude scale (Hendrick *et al.* 1998) on http://www.fetzer.org/sites/default/files/images/stories/pdf/selfmeasures/Different_Types_of_Love_LOVE_ATTITUDES_SHORT.pdf

You can complete the scale yourself and/or administer it to others.

Styles of loving: types of love and attachment styles

Hazan and Shaver (1987, 1990) argue that the kinds of attachment bonds we form in childhood influence the style of loving we experience as an adult. They hypothesise that the same kinds of individual differences observed in infants might manifest themselves among adults as reflected in their relationships. As we saw in Chapter 1, Ainsworth *et al.* (1978) proposed that, as a consequence of the way in which adults were treated as babies, infants show three *attachment styles* towards their parents: *secure, avoidant or ambivalent (anxious/insecure)*. According to Hazan and Shaver, each of these forms of attachment is related to later loving in the following ways.

- Those who showed *secure attachment* in infancy are confident in their adult relationships, find it easy to get close to people and are not unduly worried about being rejected. They are quite happy to be dependent and have people depend on them; they are trusting and stable.
- Those who were *avoidant* in infancy tend to become nervous when people get too close to them and are unwilling to depend on others. They fear that a potential partner may expect to become more intimate than they themselves would like. They are detached and unresponsive.
- Those who showed *ambivalent (anxious or insecure) attachment* in early childhood worry that their partners do not really love them, at least with the intensity they would like. These people would like to merge completely with their partner. They are anxious and uncertain.

Hazan and Shaver (1987) asked adults to select from three descriptions the one that most closely resembled the way they felt. The choices they were given were as follows:

A. I find it relatively easy to get close to others and am comfortable depending on them and having them depend on me. I don't often worry about being abandoned or about someone getting too close to me.
B. I am somewhat uncomfortable being close to others. I find it difficult to trust them completely, difficult to allow myself to depend on them. I am nervous when anyone gets too close, and love partners often want me to be more intimate than I feel comfortable being.

C. I find that others are reluctant to get as close as I would like. I often worry that my partner doesn't really love me or won't want to stay with me. I want to merge completely with another person, and this desire sometimes scares people away.

A = secure B = avoidant C = anxious/ambivalent
(from Shaver *et al.* 1988).

The respondents also answered a variety of specific questions about their experiences in romantic relationships. In general, adults with secure attachment styles found happiness, trust and friendship in their relationships. Those with the avoidant style showed a fear of intimacy and a reluctance to commit at all. Individuals with an anxious style reported experiencing extremes of emotions, including a desire for love at first sight and obsessive preoccupations with regard to the object of their desire.

In support of their theory, Hazan and Shaver point out that the percentage of the three styles of attachment found in adults approximates very closely to that found in infants: 60 per cent are secure, 20 to 25 per cent are avoidant and 15 to 20 per cent are ambivalent. Furthermore, adults with different attachment styles reported different childhood experiences that were broadly in line with what the theory would predict. Secure individuals reported positive family relationships; avoidant individuals spoke of difficulties with their mother and ambivalent people mentioned difficulties with their father (Hazan & Shaver, 1987). Hazan and Shaver argue that adult attachments, like infant ones, serve a biological purpose. Just as infant–caregiver attachment serves the survival function of keeping the baby near the adult because separation could result in death, so adult attachments are designed by evolution to bind together potential parents so that the infant will have reliable care.

How enduring are these attachment styles? Kirkpatrick and Hazan (1994) reported that 70 per cent of respondents chose the same attachment style as they had four years previously. This shows that in the majority of cases attachment style remained stable, but we must not lose sight of the fact that nearly one-third of individuals did show a change.

It is recognised that infant attachment styles are not the only influence on later relationships. Hazan herself pointed out that changes in attachment styles may be related to experience in later romantic relationships (Hazan *et al.* 1991). These researchers found that secure individuals who had experienced a disastrous relationship in adulthood were more likely to become insecure, whereas a successful romance may make individuals more secure.

Levitt (1991) argues that it is too simple to view the quality of later relationships being dependent solely on the initial parent–child attachment. People bring all sorts of expectations to a relationship (as pointed out by e.g. Argyle & Henderson 1985; Duck 1988) and have many experiences that are influential. Levitt believes that infant attachments almost certainly have an influence, but so do other factors, such as our general understanding of people, our cultural norms (such as our shared beliefs about how lovers should behave) and our personal ideologies (such as feminism or traditionalist).

In essence then, attachment styles in adult life may depend both on what we bring to a relationship and what we get from it.

Based on work by Ainsworth *et al.* (1978), Brennan *et al.* (1998) suggest that Ainsworth's three major attachment 'types' could be viewed as variations on two fundamental dimensions, these being:

- *Attachment-related anxiety* – fear of interpersonal rejection or abandonment, an excessive need for approval from others and distress when one's partner is unavailable or unresponsive.
- *Attachment related avoidance* – fear of dependence and interpersonal intimacy, an excessive need for self-reliance, and reluctance to self-disclosure.

Those high in **attachment-related anxiety** tend to worry constantly about whether their partner is responsive, attentive, available and, indeed, loves them. Those high in **attachment-related avoidance** prefer not to rely on others or to open themselves up to others; in essence, they remain aloof. A secure adult is low on both of these dimensions.

As these dimensions are independent of each other they can be combined in various ways as shown in Figure 5.4.

Thus, rather than three categories of attachment, there are four quadrants or conceptual patterns: *secure*, *preoccupied*, *fearful-avoidant* and *dismissing-avoidant*. This may also reflect infant attachment styles (see, for example, Fraley & Spieker 2003). This and other research has led theorists to suggest

> ## REFLECTIVE EXERCISE 5.2
>
> Obviously the work of Hazan and Shaver is closely related to areas of Child Psychology and attachment behaviour, so it's useful to use your knowledge of that area of psychology when considering the validity of their propositions.
>
> From your own personal experiences of your own history of attachment (which, although you won't remember them, can probably be surmised from your relationships with your mother or other main attachment figure) and your later experiences in adult romantic relationships, discuss the extent do you think that Hazan and Shaver are correct. What experiences, other than infant attachment ones, do you personally think may influence adult romantic relationships?

KEY TERMS

Attachment-related anxiety Fear of rejection, an obsessive need for approval.

Attachment-related avoidance Fear of dependence and interpersonal intimacy.

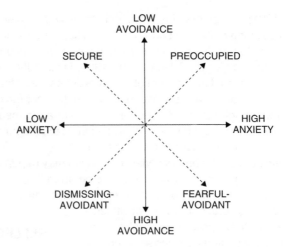

Figure 5.4 Brennan *et al.*'s (1998) four quadrants of attachment.

that individual differences in adult attachment styles can be measured on continuous dimensions rather than in categories; that they vary in degree rather than in kind.

Since time immemorial there have been theories about what love is but the development of testable theories that can be empirically validated is a relatively recent phenomenon. Sternberg (1997) comments that the variety of forms these theories take may reflect the fact that they are looking at somewhat different aspects of love: Lee's theory is one of styles of love; Sternberg's is about the actual components of love whilst Shaver and Hazan considers styles of attachment patterns in love. It may be, therefore, that these theories are not at present directly comparable but eventually there may be a time when they can be combined into a single all-embracing theory of love.

Summary

- Liking, companionate love and passionate love can be distinguished as follows:
  - Liking is the affection we feel for casual acquaintances.
  - Companionate love is the affection we feel for those with whom our lives are deeply entwined.
  - Passionate love is a powerful emotional state that involves overwhelming feelings of tenderness, elation, anxiety and sexual desire.

- Rubin devised scales by which to measure Liking and Loving:
  - o The liking scale looks at similarity to oneself and respect for the other person.
  - o The loving scale measures attachment, caring and intimacy.
- Sternberg's triangular theory of love proposes that love comprises three components: intimacy, passion and commitment. They interact with each other to provide eight different types of love.
- Lee's 'Colours of Love' typology suggests that there are three basic styles of loving (just as there are three primary colours): eros, ludus and storge. In a comparable way that primary colours combine to make other colours, these combine to give three secondary styles: mania, pragma and agape.
- Hazan and Shaver (1987, 1990) propose that the individual differences shown in infant attachment behaviour, that is, secure, avoidant-insecure and ambivalent-insecure correspond to adult styles of loving. Others (e.g. Levitt 1991) argue that later relationships are not solely dependent on initial infant–carer attachment but on later experiences and expectations.

FURTHER READING

Brennan, K.A. & Shaver, P.R. (1998) Attachment styles and personality disorders: Their connections to each other and to parental divorce, parental death, and perceptions of parental caregiving. *Journal of Personality*, *66*, 835–878

Hendrick, C. & Hendrick, S. (1989) Research on love: Does it measure up? *Journal of Personality and Social Psychology*, *56*, 784–94. [This article considers whether the measures of love (the love instruments) actually measure what they purport to measure.]

Lee, J.A. (1973) *Colours of Love: An Exploration of the Ways of Loving.* Toronto: New Press.

Regan, P. (2011). *Close Relationships* (Chapter 10). New York: Routledge.

Simpson, J.A. & Rholes, W.S. (Eds.) (1998) *Attachment Theory and Close Relationships* (Chapter 1). New York: Guilford Press.

Sternberg, R.J. (1986) A triangular theory of love. *Psychological Review*, *93*(2), 119–135.

Types of relationships
1 – friendship and kinship

6

What this chapter will teach you

- How relationships can be classified.

- What we mean by 'close' relationships.

- The variation in the way in which parent–child relationships can be classified.

- The characteristics of sibling relationships.

- What friendship is, how friendship changes with age; characteristics of same-sex and cross-sex friendships; gender differences in friendship.

- The influence of the internet on relationships.

Classification of relationships

We experience a significant number of relationships in our lives. For many of us, the first principal ones are those with our parents and other close relatives. As we grow up, other relationships become important: we make friends, we go to work, we have romantic liaisons – all of these everyday life events involve interpersonal interactions which greatly influence the quality of our lives.

Because there is such a variety of relationships, it is useful to have a system by which they can be classified. One such system categorises relationships according to two main dimensions: one dimension reflects the degree of closeness and the other expresses the extent to which the relationship is one of choice.

Personal vs. social dimension

The degree of closeness, intimacy and interdependence of a relationship is an obvious way in which it can be described. Relationships high on closeness can be referred to as *personal* whilst those at the low end of this dimension would be considered to be *social.* A more detailed consideration of what is meant by closeness is examined shortly.

Voluntary vs. non-voluntary dimension

Another common distinction in relationships is expressed in the saying 'you can chose your friends but you can't choose your family', that is, it distinguishes between those relationships that are voluntary and those that are imposed on us by exogenous (outside) factors. Voluntary relationships, such as friendship and mating relationships, are mainly dependent on internal factors such as the degree to which people like each other and people are relatively free to choose such relationships. These are contrasted with ones that are forced on people by circumstances such as work and family; these include parent–child, student–teacher and co-workers. Unlike voluntary relationships, these involuntary ones do not depend on the degree of liking between the two parties.

Since these two main dimensions are independent of each other, they can combine in any way: we can have close relationships that were developed by circumstances (non-voluntary) and fairly impersonal relationships with people with whom we choose to mix. One way of representing this is shown in Table 6.1.

Table 6.1 Voluntary and involuntary relationships

	Personal relationships	*Social relationships*
Voluntary	Marriage Cohabiting couples Best friend	Acquaintances Casual friends Relational marketing
Involuntary *(exogenous)*	Parent–child Siblings Grandparent–child	Distant relatives Work relationships Monopoly provider–client

The dimension of 'closeness'

We often hear people talk about having a close relationship with some-one, but what does this mean? (Before reading on, perhaps you'd like to consider this from your own personal perspective.) Let's consider three different approaches to defining 'closeness' in the context of a relationship.

Degree of interdependence

Berscheid *et al.* (1989) suggested that closeness is related to the *degree of interdependence* between two people. Interdependence means that each partner's thoughts, emotions and behaviour influence the other's. There are three main types of interdependence: cognitive, behavioural and affective.

1   Cognitive interdependence involves *thinking* of you and your partner as inextricably linked rather than as separate individuals (Agnew *et al.* 1998) ('she's my best friend'; 'I couldn't live without him').
2   Behavioural interdependence means that each has an influence over the other's activities, decisions and plans. The partners usually spend a lot of time together and share a number of different activities. Interestingly, the extent of behavioural interdependence is a strong predictor of how long a relationship will last, even stronger than a couple's positive feelings for each other (Berscheid *et al.* 1989).
3   Affective interdependence refers to how the partners feel about each other. These feelings are usually positive but some relation-ships, especially non-voluntary ones, can involve strong negative emotions. Whether positive or negative, affective interdepend-ence means that each partner's emotional well-being is affected by what the other does.

The more frequent, diverse and strong the impact of each person's thoughts, feelings and behaviour on the other and the longer the rela-tionship has lasted, the closer it is. Although all three types of **interde-pendence** are important aspects of relationships, the degree to which these three are present in any particular rela-tionship will vary.

Intimacy and support

Another approach draws a parallel between closeness and **intimacy**, that is, the extent to which two people understand, support and care for one another (Reis & Patrick 1996).

KEY TERMS

Interdependence In a relationship, the degree to which each partner's thoughts, emotions and behaviour influ-ences the other's.

Intimacy The extent to which two people understand, support and care for one another.

Alongside this goes a similar one that equates closeness with *the degree of motivation to respond supportively to the other's welfare*, to spend time, effort, money and invest emotionally in order to benefit the partner (Mills *et al.* 2004).

Security and welfare

Clark and Lemay (2010) define closeness of a relationship in terms of the degree to which it serves two broad functions: firstly, to provide both members with a sense of security that their welfare is protected and enhanced by their partner and will continue to be; secondly, to provide both members with a sense that they are responsive to one another's welfare and will continue to be.

Types of close relationships

Relationships with relations

For the vast majority of people, relationships with our family members, especially with our parents and children, are a vital feature of our social network from the cradle to the grave. However much they may at times cause intense irritation (drive us nuts!), our families serve a vital function in our lives, providing us with a shared identity and a safe base.

Despite the popular stereotype of the isolated nuclear family in the Western world, links between family members in different geographical households are often very close – especially in these days of telephones, faxes and e-mails. Finch and Mason (1993) found that the majority of adults have some contact with their mothers at least once a week and over 10 per cent see them daily. No matter how great the distance between parents and children, links remain strong, the strongest typically being with mothers. There is a sense of obligation to remain in touch with all immediate family members, but especially with parents. However, this sense of obligation does not detract from the fact that links are also maintained through mutual enjoyment – we do not only keep in touch because we 'have to' but because we want to.

Here we take a more detailed look at two sets of relationships with family members: parent–child relationships and sibling relationships.

Parent–child relationships

Children are brought up within families, both nuclear and extended, and when discussing a parent–child relationship it is essential to bear in mind that it cannot be considered in isolation. Since the relationship is formed within the context of the wider family it is profoundly influenced by the whole family dynamics. **Systems theory** (Sameroff 1994) places emphasis on the family as a social system and recognises that, in order to understand the nature of parent–child relationship, it is necessary to recognise the interdependence of all family members (Parke 2004). Parke *et al.* (2006) document three approaches to classifying the impact of parent–child relationships on children's later personality and behaviour: the typological approach, the attachment approach and the parent–child interactional approach.

The typological approach: Early research tended to classify parent–child relationships in terms of child-rearing practices. Baumrind (1973) distinguished three types of parental child-rearing practices: authoritarian, authoritative and permissive. The **authoritarian** parent expects children to obey strict rules without question and punishes any failure to do so. The **authoritative** parent establishes rules and guidelines but is willing to discuss them with the child and negotiate; they use a more democratic style, consider the child's wishes and avoid use of harsh punishment. **Permissive** parents have few rules, indulge their children's whims, rarely punish them and have low expectations of self-control or self-discipline. Authoritative parenting was believed to provide the optimum environment as it was associated with children who had good emotional adjustment and high self-confidence whilst authoritarian upbringing, especially for boys, had negative consequences such as low levels of cognitive and social competence, unfriendliness and lack of self-esteem (Baumrind 1991).

Systems theory has criticised this 'typology' approach on the grounds that it places too much emphasis on the parental style of the relationship. It is quite possible that the child's temperament and/or behaviour has influenced the parental style rather than the other way around. It is not difficult to imagine that a wilful, obstinate and aggressive child may lead even the most liberal minded parent to become so frustrated and exasperated that they resort to an authoritarian style ('Do as you're told NOW!'), especially if they are behaving in a way that could be dangerous.

A different type of criticism questions whether the negative effect of an authoritarian child-rearing style is universal: cross-ethnic studies indicate that it is essential to take account of the cultural context.

KEY TERMS

Systems theory A theory of relationships that argues that it is necessary to recognise the interdependence of all family members in order to understand parent–child relationships.

Authoritarian child-rearing style Children are expected to obey strict rules, given little autonomy, harshly punished.

Authoritative child-rearing style Children are given guidelines and rules which they expected to follow but are open to discussion. They are given a degree of autonomy.

Permissive child-rearing style Children are given few guidelines or rules and are indulged; there are low expectations of self-control or self-discipline.

Two different examples serve to make this point. The first example is concerned with the essence of what is involved in authoritarianism. Chao (1994) argues that Chinese mothers have a different set of child-rearing values and styles from the traditional American/European child-rearing schemes and it is not possible to directly compare the two. What may appear to be an authoritarian style in Chinese families is not the equivalent in Western ones with far more emphasis on ambition for the child's success in the Chinese family. The second example questions the assumption that authoritative upbringing is preferable to authoritarianism regardless of circumstance. When children are reared in, for example, dangerous and threatening ecological environments, the authoritarian style in which children unquestioning obey a parent may be more practical and therefore positive than one in which children have greater self-determination (Baldwin *et al.* 1990).

DISCUSS AND DEBATE

'The view that the authoritative style of parenting is the optimum one is ethnocentric'. Discuss.

The attachment approach: Another way of classifying parent–child relationships is on the basis of attachment theory (Bowlby 1969/1982, 1973). As discussed in previous chapters, Ainsworth *et al.* (1978) proposed that, as a consequence of the way in which parents treat their children, infants show three attachment styles towards their parents: *secure, avoidant or ambivalent (anxious/insecure)* (see Chapter 1). These styles are formed in infancy but have an enduring influence on relationships throughout life. For example, compared with insecurely attached children, securely attached ones are more likely to have close family relationships, long-term friendships, sustained romantic involvement, higher self-confidence and greater determination with respect to achieving important goals. Attachment styles reflect people's beliefs about the nature of relationships in general and their feelings and evaluation of their current relationships (Baldwin 1992). Securely attached people are the most likely of the three attachment types to find happiness, satisfaction and trust in relationships and have highest self-esteem. Those who are avoidant fear closeness and tend to be less accepting of their partners. The anxiously attached have a tendency towards jealousy, passion and anger.

To summarise, attachment styles influence both people's trust in their partner's support and responsiveness and their own willingness to offer support. Securely attached individuals derive the highest satisfaction from their relationships in the long term compared with avoidant or anxious individuals (Collins & Read 1990).

Attachment theory continues to be an influential approach which predicts other relationships such as friendship and adult romantic relationships (as discussed in the previous chapter). In the cross-cultural context it has provided the basis for new insights into how culture-specific experiences shape the nature of dominant attachment patterns in different cultures (Van Ijzendoorn & Sagi 1999). Nevertheless, it is again necessary to use a family-systems perspective to fully appreciate the ways in which mother, father and sibling attachment patterns interact to affect a child's developmental outcomes; the emphasis should not be focused entirely on the caregiver–child relationship.

The parent–child interactional approach emphasises the importance of day to day interactions between parent and child in helping the child acquire basic social skills that eventually lead to successful social interaction. It overlaps with the

attachment approach in focusing mainly on parent–child interaction patterns in shaping an infant's development but centres on specific aspects of parent–child exchanges on a continuum rather than trying to classify the interactions into types (secure, insecure etc.). Important findings in this approach include the following. Warm responsive parents are more likely to have children who are socially competent (Grimes *et al.* 2004) and adjust well to school (Harrist *et al.* 1994). This approach, unlike the attachment approach, looks specifically at fathers whose influence is separate and important, though not as strong as that of mothers (Hart *et al.* 1998). Carson and Parke (1996) found that when fathers react negatively to their preschool children's negative behaviour the children become more aggressive and less altruistic than their peers. Mothers do not have this effect. This suggests that fathers have more influence than do mothers in how children handle their negative emotions.

Like attachment theory, this theory has stood the test of time and been influential in understanding parent–child relationships. Nevertheless, it has been criticised for its failure to take sufficient account of genetic and biological factors such as temperament (Plomin 1994). Another important shortcoming, as with attachment theory, is its failure to take sufficient account of the whole family interaction, especially the way in which the mother's and father's influence combine to affect the child's development. Finally, it needs to take greater account of how cultural beliefs and practices influence parent–child interaction.

DISCUSS AND DEBATE

As a child, how did your relationship with your mother differ from your relationship with your father? Did they use different parenting styles? Is it possible to say that one had more influence on you than the other or were they simply different influences? How did their influences *combine* to affect your development?

Sibling relationships

Sibling relationships are, and always have been, of enormous importance to children and adolescents (and, some would add, to adults) the world over. For most individuals the sibling relationship is the longest lasting relationship in their lives (Ponzetti & James 1997). It has been estimated that approximately 80% of the population spends at least one-third of their lives with their siblings (Fitzpatrick & Badzinski 1994). Sibling interaction is a part of daily routine: in many families children spend more time with siblings than with any other companions. Unique roles and functions exist in these relationships: brothers and sisters act as confidants, role-models, socialisation agents and caretakers (Campbell *et al.* 1999). They also provide financial, emotional and moral support for each other (Goetting 1986).

That said, it is not all moonlight and roses! As virtually all parents know, the stereotype of the love–hate relationship between siblings is well founded: they can go from best friends to hated enemies in an instant. Observational studies indicate that conflict can occur up to eight times an hour (e.g. Dunn & Munn 1986) and surveys indicate that physical violence between siblings takes place in 70% of families (e.g. Straus *et al.* 1980). It's no wonder that sibling relationships are a main concern of parents! One reason for the constant switching between warmth and conflict may be because the relationship is non-voluntary: the children have not chosen these companions and they cannot choose to put a physical distance between them for any length of time, if at all. At the same time, this relationship is one of emotional intensity, hence the strong feelings it evokes.

It has been suggested that there are several dimensions on which sibling relationships can be distinguished: the amount of contact, the intensity of emotion and the role-structure. The first two speak for themselves. In terms of contact, some siblings spend little time together, especially if there is a large age gap and very different interests whereas others share a bedroom and are together a great deal of the time. Some sibling relationships are very emotionally intense, others are indifferent. Some are extremely positive, less often they are extremely negative. Most are a mixture of both. To some extent this depends on temperament but it also depends on the age gap and sex of the individuals.

In terms of role-structure, we can identify two different relationships: *complementary* and *egalitarian*. In egalitarian relationships, the siblings are equal and serve the same role. A complementary relationship is one typified by a 'parent–child' relationship: one sibling acts as a parent and takes a caring role. The amount of complementarity differs significantly among cultures. In some societies older girls are the main caregivers. In adolescents the complementary role becomes important in many Western families in which older adolescents act as a role-model (not necessarily a good one) and a source of advice and information for younger siblings.

Friendship

What is friendship?

Although we all know what a friend is, it is a surprisingly difficult term to define. Duck (1991) comments that a friend of his once suggested that a friend was a person who, seeing you drunk and about to get up on a table and sing, would quietly take you take aside to prevent you from doing it. As Duck says, this definition embodies quite a few important aspects of what constitutes a friend: someone who cares, supports, is loyal, and who puts a high priority on the other person's interests. Another essential characteristic of a friend is that they are someone you like and who likes you. Perhaps the essence of friendship is the feeling of comfort, of freedom and naturalness of emotion.

DISCUSS AND DEBATE

It is an obvious fact, but one that is sometimes overlooked, that whatever your situation in terms of siblings, you cannot have experienced what any other situation is like. So, if you were brought up as one of five children (as was the author) you can have no concept of what it is like to be an only child. As well as the number of children in the family, age differences, combinations of girls and boys and so on make each experience within a family unique. There is also the issue of step-siblings, half-siblings and suchlike to add to the variety, not to mention adopted single children and sibling groups. Discuss your own experiences within a group of people. Try not to make stereotyped assumptions ('all only children are spoilt') but actually listen to other people's experiences and consider the advantages, disadvantages and general influences of different family structures as applied to sibling relationships.

A more formal definition of friendship is offered by Hays (1988, p. 395) 'A voluntary interdependence between two persons over time, that is intended to facilitate social-emotional goals of the participants, and may involve varying types and degrees of companionship, intimacy, affection and mutual assistance'. This definition emphasises the fact that the primary motivation for forming a friendship is *social-emotional*, to provide companionship and emotional support rather than *instrumental* (the achievement of specific goals). As Wright (1984) comments, a friend is a person whose company we enjoy for his or her own sake rather than for the things he or she does.

Friendship is universal: at all ages, in all classes and cultures, men and women, boys and girls, form bonds of friendship. In adults it is characterised by a number of features such as self-disclosure, trust, interpersonal perception and commitment. Friends make a huge contribution to our welfare: they are an important source of meaning, love, happiness, enjoyment and excitement in our lives. Indeed friendship is one of life's most essential and rewarding forms of interaction.

Argyle and Henderson (1985) outlined the norms and rules that are most important in friendship. Friends freely help in times of need; they trust and respect each other and share confidences while respecting each other's privacy. They do not criticise each other in public and will not tolerate others being unpleasant about friends who are not there to defend themselves.

Changes in friendship with age

There is considerable variation both in the degree of intimacy and in the stability of friendships. Childhood friendships tend to be fairly unstable, while those made during adolescence and early adulthood are often the closest and most enduring.

Friendships take different forms and serve different purposes at various stages of life. Although preschool children show more intimate behaviour with some peers than with others, at this age they have no concept of friendship as an enduring kind of relationship: friends are essentially playmates.

From about the age of 8, children begin to see friends as people who can be trusted to be loyal, kind, cooperative and sensitive to the other's needs (Pataki *et al.* 1994). In adolescence there is an emphasis on friends being people who truly understand each other's strengths and

Figure 6.1 Friendship is very important in the teenage years.

weaknesses and are willing to confide their innermost feelings (Hartup 1992). During adolescence, same-sex friendships are probably more intense than at any other age.

As people grow older and marry, friendship becomes less central to their lives and not as close. Adults tend to draw their friends from the immediate neighbourhood and from work; these relationships are usually less intimate than those based on early attachments (Argyle & Henderson 1985).

Contrary to popular belief, most older people (those above the age of 60) are not lonely and friendless; the vast majority have at least one close friend. Friends in late adulthood provide intimacy, people with whom to share activities, and are a source of excitement and joy (Adams 1986). Friends are especially important to elderly women who are more likely to be widowed than men.

Same-sex and cross-sex friendship

Friends tend to be similar in terms of age, education and sex, with opposite-sex friendships being much less common than same-sex ones. This starts in early childhood and although some of it may be due to social norms, Maccoby (1990) cites evidence that children find same-sex play partners more compatible than opposite sex ones. Whiting and Edwards (1988) reported from their observations of six different cultures (India, Japan, Kenya, Mexico, the Philippines and the USA) that same-sex preferences emerge in all cultures at similar ages and is quite well established by 6 years of age.

Despite this, there is evidence that children's preference for same-sex friendships may, at least in part, be due to social pressure. Many observations are made in schools, but when children are observed playing and talking outside the school setting in their neighbourhood or in their homes, the picture that emerges may be very different. Dunn (2004) reports that Rogoff *et al.* (cited by Ellis *et al.* 1981) observed US children playing in groups and found almost the same percentage of mixed as same-sex groups. Even in children over the age of 8 there was a lot of mixing of gender. In poor areas of London a similar pattern emerges with boys and girls in early adolescence regularly congregating on street corners whereas at school they mixed predominantly in same-sex groups. Cross-gender friendships rarely survive in school. Dunn (2004) quotes 7-year-old Katy who had been friends with Jake all her life and still played with him outside school. When asked why they didn't mix in school she said 'We'd both get teased. He doesn't want to be called "sissy" – and we both hate jokes about kissing and stuff ...' (p. 115).

With respect to adults, many lovers are also friends, so the distinction between lovers and friends is not an easy one to make. However, cross-sex friendships that involve no physical intimacy are less common than same-sex ones, especially among married people. Several reasons have been suggested for this. There are strong social pressures on people not to engage in such relationships; expressions like 'we're just good friends' are viewed with scepticism. These relationships are not only seen as threatening to intimate relationships, they are also viewed with suspicion by co-workers and others who see them as inevitably potentially sexual. In addition, opportunities for men and women to meet on equal terms are less common than for such same-sex encounters. According to Sapadin (1988) adult women rate cross-sex relationships lower than same-sex relationships on scales of overall quality, intimacy, enjoyment and nurturance. In contrast, men rate them more highly on all these dimensions except intimacy, which is rated the same. Both sexes believed that cross-sex friendships provided them with new understandings and perspectives of the opposite sex.

Gender differences in friendship

From an early age and throughout life there are significant sex differences in styles of friendships. The main gender difference in such friendships is neatly expressed by Wright (1982) as 'side-by-side' for male–male as opposed to 'face-to-face' for female–female. More formally, the differences have been labelled *instrumental* versus *expressive*. **Instrumental friendships** are those based on a sharing of activities; **expressive friendships** are those based on the sharing of emotions.

> **KEY TERMS**
>
> **Instrumental friendships** Friendships based on common activities.
>
> **Expressive friendships** Friendships based on sharing of emotions.

As already mentioned, sex segregation in friendship starts early. At around age 3 or 4, children show a preference for same-sex peers with whom to play and by age 9 or 10, as many of us will recall from our own childhood, it is an insult to suggest that a boy likes a girl.

In the school playground boys are inclined to play in large mixed-age groups, while girls are more often in smaller groups or same-sex pairs. Boys tend to play competitive team games that involve skills of cooperation, competition and leadership, whereas the activities enjoyed by girls tend to emphasise intimacy and exclusiveness (Lever, 1978). Dunn (2004) refers to boys' friendships as *extensive* in its networks of playmates whilst girls' friendships are *intensive*, consisting of smaller-scale groups or 'cliques'.

With regard to adults, the patterns are essentially the same as those begun in childhood. Unger and Crawford (1992) reviewed several studies which showed that, compared to men's friendships, those between women tended to be more intimate, more intense and generally more important to the people involved. Several theorists suggest that women use friendship as a means to confide in each other. For women, getting together with friends often takes the form of asking them over for coffee to discuss personal matters. In contrast, men tend to choose friends from people with whom they share a mutual interest, so that they can enjoy joint activities such as fishing, watching football or playing a game of badminton (Sherrod 1989). Women in general have higher expectation of friends than do men and place greater emphasis on intimacy (Felmlee & Muraco 2009). Hayduk (1983) points out that men's competitiveness is inconsistent with sharing confidences, which may be a reason for their reluctance to do so. Interestingly, Rawlins (1992) suggests that, although competition is often central to the joint activities undertaken within male friendships, the *social interaction* in which they engage as part of these activities is often more important than winning or losing. It is almost as if men need an excuse to interact with each other, and this excuse is a joint activity which is enjoyable in itself but not the sole purpose of its existence.

Reis *et al.* (1985) believe that these differences are not due to men's inability to be intimate; no differences between men and women are evident in their social skills. When requested by researchers to join in intimate conversations, men are quite as capable of doing this as are women and they are also able to judge from video fragments the different degrees of intimacy in a relationship. Reis *et al.* conclude that,

DISCUSS AND DEBATE

In a mixed group of men and women/ boys and girls, discuss whether, in your experience, same-sex friendships between men and women differ in the ways described above.

(a)   (b)

Figure 6.2a & b Are men's friendships 'side-by-side' whilst women's are 'face-to-face'?

should they so choose, men can have just as intimate interactions as women – but they prefer not to.

Socio-evolutionary theory argues that there are sound reasons why evolution favours the selection of 'instrumental' relationships between men and 'emotionally expressive' relationships between women. Based on work with chimpanzees, De Waal (1983) suggests that, in order to survive, it was necessary for males to undertake joint activities so that they could collaborate in hunting and fighting. Females, on the other hand, needed to be able to establish a supportive, nurturing network aimed at caring for the infants. This theory is largely speculative and overlooks the role of socialisation in favour of biology. In the main, studies suggest that both are important. The family, school and media all appear to play an important part in shaping behaviour, but some fundamental differences between men and women appear to persist despite different social and cultural influences.

Traditionally, researchers have drawn our attention to the differences rather than the similarities in male and female same-sex friendships. However, Duck and Wright (1993) contend that these differences may have been somewhat exaggerated. They have re-analysed earlier research findings and suggest that although women and men differ on a number of variables, the differences did not correspond to an instrumental versus expressive dichotomy. For example, when asked to give the reasons why they arranged to meet their friends, both men and women reported that they met most often just to talk, less often to engage in mutual activities and least often to deal with a relationship issue. Expressive and instrumental characteristics were about equally prominent aspects of a strong friendship for both men and women. Duck and Wright contend that both men and women are caring, supportive and encouraging in their relationships, but women are likely to express these feelings more openly. According to these researchers, just because, compared to women, men do not engage in such explicit displays of affection and personal disclosure does not mean that their friendships are any less emotional. In support of this, Felmlee and Muraco (2009), despite finding that women place greater emphasis on intimacy than do men (as mentioned earlier), nevertheless found that both sexes share similar norms for friendship – those of trust, commitment and respect.

Internet relationships

One of the biggest cultural changes in recent years is associated with the use of communication by social media, i.e. virtual communities and networks. However did we manage without the internet and mobile phones? Email, Facebook, MySpace, YouTube, Twitter, texting are all now an indispensable part of our everyday lives. Even grandparents (most of them anyway) don't go out without their mobile phone and half of teenagers have an online profile (Lenhart & Madden [2007] of the Pew Internet and Life Project). Such means of communication has rapidly become part of modern life and the new and old have become integrated with people moving between phone, email and face-to-face contact.

Wellman (2001) uses the term 'networked individualism' to depict his view that society has moved away from a form of social organisation in which we belonged to and interacted within small densely knit groups to one in which we interact on an individual basis with other individuals. In other words, in the 'old days' people were born into a small tightly-knit community in which they lived, worked and eventually died. Communication was mainly face-to-face from one household to another. Nowadays individuals, rather than households, are separately connected via the internet and cell phone, and communication has moved from house-to-house to person-to-person. Hence the term **networked individualism** to express the fact that rather than being part of a single community, people are part of many communities and actively seek out a variety of people and resources for different situa-

KEY TERM

Networked individualism The tendency for people to interact on an individual-to-individual basis of people networked together rather than interacting on a group-to-group basis within a tightly knit community.

tions. The implication of this is that interpersonal relationships become more and more based on specialised roles: particular interests, common goals or problems, need for information. People may be members of many discussion forums and dip in and out as they please.

What effect does this have on relationships? One side of the argument is that it has expanded our relationships, both socially and geographically and made it far easier to maintain meaningful relationships despite inevitable separations. The other side is that people are becoming alienated from close, rich, authentic relationships while they forge superficial (sometimes dishonest) relationships with strangers – that staring at a computer screen whilst 'chatting' has replaced looking at someone's face in a real-world situation. This expresses the worry that the relationships that exist in text are less satisfying than those in which people can really see and touch each other.

Boase *et al.* (2006) of the Pew Internet and Life Project, address several issues with regard to the internet's impact on relationships. They report that rather than destroying person to person relationships, the internet is enabling people to maintain existing ties and often to strengthen them, as well as using the internet to form new ones. Grandma can now email her grandchildren in New Zealand from her sitting room in Kent; she can also talk to them and see them on Skype. Chris, who only saw Louise a couple of hours ago at school, can text and ask her to pop round for tea so they can do some homework together. Via Facebook and other social media sites Lewis can keep in touch with old school friends across the globe. Online and offline relationships, rather than being separate as some people had once feared, are well integrated. Much of the communication that takes place online is with the same set of friends and family who are also contacted in person and by phone. According to Boase and Wellman (2006), a relatively small minority of internet users actually use the internet to communicate with people they do not already know from their everyday lives and the few people who do forge new relationships online soon meet them in person and therefore integrate them into their offline life. Rather than email reducing the amount of other contact we have, the opposite is true: the more people contact others by email, the more they use the phone or make person to person contact (Chen & Wellman 2003). Furthermore, more friendships are initiated and maintained in an offline context, i.e. the 'real world', than an online one (Buote *et al.* 2009). Neither does it appear that email has reduced the significance of geography – our friends are still those who live nearby. In the US, 91% of teenagers using social networking sites (SNS) say they use it to keep in touch with friends they meet often (Lenhart & Madden 2007). In the UK, most online communication made by children aged 9–19 is with local friends (Livingstone & Bober 2005). Across a range of ages in the US, 31% of people said that the internet had increased the number of their significant ties whilst only 2% reported that it had decreased them. It would be fair to conclude then that, far from destroying meaningful relationships, the internet has increased and strengthened them.

Summary

- Close relationships can be classified in terms of two dimensions: the personal versus social dimension and voluntary versus non-voluntary dimension.
- Closeness in a relationship can be defined as the degree of interdependence between two people. Types of interdependence are

  o cognitive (the extent to which you think of you and your partner as being linked).

- o Behavioural (how much you and your partner do together).
- o Affective (how you and your partner feel about each other).

- Systems theory argues that it is necessary to recognise the interdependence of all family members in order to understand parent–child relationships. Parke *et al.* (2006) suggest that the impact of parent–child relationships on children's later personality can be classified according to three approaches: the typological approach (based on child-rearing practices); the attachment approach; and the parent–child interaction approach. All of these approaches have merit but have been criticised for not taking sufficient account of a child's innate temperament. They also concentrate on one relationship (e.g. mother–child) and fail to take full account of whole family interactions.
- Sibling relationships are the longest lasting relationships in many people's lives. During childhood and sometimes into adulthood they involve intense emotions, both positive and negative. They can be distinguished in terms of amount of contact, intensity of emotion and role-structure.
- Friends are people you like and who like you; friendship is one of the most rewarding forms of interaction.

  - o Friendships change with age – they are very unstable in young children, very intense during adolescence and less central and intimate during adulthood.
  - o Same-sex friendships are more common than cross-sex ones. This appears to be the norm within most cultures implying that the preference is biologically based. However, there are social pressures that discourage cross-sex friendships both in children and adults.
  - o There are gender differences in friendship with female–female being 'face-to-face' while male–male is 'side-by-side'. Some psychologists (e.g. Duck & Wright 1993) contend that these differences are exaggerated. Felmlee and Muraco (2009) point out that both sexes share similar norms of trust, commitment and respect.

- The internet has had considerable affect on relationships, particularly friendship.

o Wellman (2001) uses the term 'networked individualism' to depict his view that society has moved away from a form of social organisation in which we belonged to and interacted within small densely knit groups to one in which we interact on an individual basis with other individuals.

o Despite fears that the social media has replaced 'real' relationships with relatively impersonal, anonymous ones, online and offline friendships appear to be well integrated. Most media communication simply strengthens existing real-life relationships rather than replacing them.

FURTHER READING

Feeney, J. & Noller, P. (1996) *Adult Attachments*. Thousand Oaks, CA: Sage.

Mesch, G.S. & Talmud, I. (2010) *Wired Youth: The Social World of Adolescence in the Information Age* (Chapters 1 and 4). New York: Routledge.

Ponzetti, J. & James, C. (1997) Loneliness and sibling relationships. *Journal of Social Behavior and Personality, 12*, 103–112.

The Pew Internet Life Project. Available from http://www.pewinternet.org/ [This is an online resource. There are many papers (see the chapter for specific references).]

Types of relationships

2 – loving and mating

7

What this chapter will teach you

- The definition and frequency across cultures of different mating systems in humans including monogamy, polygyny and polyandry.

- The basis of arranged marriages.

- The recent trends in marriage and other mating arrangements.

- The ways in which homosexual relationships can be legalised. Similarity and differences between homosexual and heterosexual relationships.

I think most people would agree that one of the most important decisions we make in life is with whom we will share it in an intimate manner. Choosing a mate is one of the most basic of human endeavours and one with the most profound consequences. Romantic relationships, also referred to as mating relationships, differ in significant ways from other close relationships. They provide love, affection, sexual activity, social support and, above all, an emotional intimacy which is not usually found in other relationships, however close. They are full of swings of emotion at all the extremes and far more immediately intense than other relationships. They can produce ecstasy when things are going well and despair when going badly.

More than any other relationships, romantic ones such as marriage are governed by social norms, expectations, and rules that regulate the partners' union. Whereas there is rarely anything that denotes the start or end of a friendship, there are all manner of rituals associated with a romantic relationship. People 'date', get engaged, get married, perhaps get divorced. Each stage has certain 'rules' which vary across different cultures and sub-cultures and which often remain unwritten and implicit, but which everyone is aware of and controlled by, even if they do not always follow them. Just think about how people might behave on a first date, or what happens when people become engaged or start living together and you will appreciate how different is the development of a romantic relationship compared with a friendship.

In all societies, there is the facility to formalise a sexual relationship: marriage is a cultural universal (Daly & Wilson 1983). In most cultures this is a legally binding contract between the two parties and there are conditions to be met before a couple can legally marry (or divorce). There are societal rules involved in marriage, such as the number of spouses an individual is permitted at any one time, the age at which it is allowed and the degree of consanguinity between the pair-bond.

Across the animal kingdom there is a large variety of mating patterns. In some species, such as in many birds, one male and one female pair for a season and share the rearing of the young. In other species, such as the red deer, one male has a harem whilst the vast majority of males are forced into virtual celibacy. Animals' mating patterns are closely related to both ecological conditions and the amount of care needed to raise the young. Although there is a wide variety of mating patterns across vertebrates, in most of these species there is only one mating system. In humans, this is not the case and the range of mating systems is diverse. The four major ones shown across cultures are:

- **Monogamy** – a marriage system between one man and one woman.
- **Polygyny** – a marriage system in which one man has several wives
- **Polyandry** – a marriage system in which one woman has several husbands
- **Polygynandry** (also called cenogamy) – a marriage system involving several males and females in one household, sharing the same spouses.

(Polygyny, polyandry and polygynandry are sometimes referred to collectively as polygamy).

Polygyny is permitted in the majority of cultures. Based on a study of 862 societies across the world, in a special edition of the *Ethnographic Atlas*, Murdock (1967) reported that over 80% of societies permit a man to take several wives and only 16% prescribe monogamy. In practice, however, even in cultures where men are permitted more than one wife, few are actually polygynous due the

KEY TERMS

Monogamy A marriage system between one man and one woman.

Polygyny A marriage system in which one man has several wives.

Polyandry A marriage system in which one woman has several husbands.

Polygynandry A marriage system involving several males and females in one household, sharing the same spouses (also called cenogamy).

extra financial and social responsibilities involved, including the large number of potential children that may result. Worldwide, there is only a small minority of men who are sufficiently wealthy and powerful to acquire and maintain multiple wives.

Polyandry is extremely rare: it is permitted in less than 1% of societies and never without polygyny also being allowed. The most common form of polyandry is fraternal polyandry in which brothers share a wife (or wives). An example of this is found amongst the Pahari brothers in India who pool resources to secure a wife whom they share. A woman goes through a marriage ceremony with the eldest brother and is then married to all the brothers; more wives may eventually be taken, again in a ceremony with the eldest brother, but they are always shared by the brothers none of whom have exclusive rights over them (Berreman 1962). If more wives are taken in this way, the living arrangement then becomes an example of *polygynandry*.

In terms of evolutionary theory, it makes little biological sense for men to have a polyandrous relationship since they cannot increase the number of children they have and their gene pool by so doing. Nevertheless, there are conditions in which it might be expedient. Fraternal polyandry can maintain the patrimonial inheritance in one piece rather than it being split among the different groups of heirs of the brothers, thereby reducing fragmentation of property. It keeps the adult to child ratio high and the number of heirs low; this could be important in situations in which the property on which the livelihood of the community depends (e.g. land) is scarce and limited. However, it is certainly not true that these conditions exist in all polyandrous communities: for example, the Pahari are no less economically secure than many people in North India, despite their reputation for being poor. What is true is that the origins of polyandry cannot be explained in the same terms everywhere and that there are complex social, cultural and historical reasons for its existence, which are not always easily understood (Berreman 1962).

Because of the genetic advantages of polygyny for men and because it is permitted in many societies, some anthropologists argue that it is the natural mating pattern for humans. Others disagree and believe that man is essentially a monogamous primate, polygyny being simply a secondary opportunistic strategy. One advocate of the latter position is Helen Fisher who points to the evidence, mentioned above, that although polygyny is permitted in the vast majority of societies, it is practiced in very few. She quotes the anthropologist Murdock (1949) who, after surveying 250 cultures, concluded 'An impartial observer employing the criterion of numerical preponderance, consequently, would be compelled to characterise nearly every known human society as monogamous, despite the preference for and frequency of polygyny in the overwhelming majority' (quoted in Fisher 1992, p. 69).

DISCUSS AND DEBATE

Given the evolutionary arguments put forward in Chapter 4 and the huge percentage of cultures that permit polygyny, discuss whether or not you agree with Helen Fisher's contention that monogamy is natural in humans. Alternatively, organise a formal debate on it with proposers and seconders from each side.

Cultural differences in choosing marriage partners

There are huge variations in the way in which marriage partners are chosen in different cultures. One of the most important sources of cultural variation in social behaviour is based on a difference first outlined by Hofstede (1984) between **individualistic** and **collectivist** cultures. The major differences between such societies can be conveniently summarised as follows.

Individualistic cultures, which include most Western nations, place the major emphasis on:

- self-interest and the interest of one's immediate family;
- personal autonomy (making your own decisions);
- individual initiative, individual achievement and independence.

Collectivist societies, which include most Eastern nations, place the major emphasis on:

- loyalty to the group that in turn looks after the interest of its members;
- interdependence;
- the belief that group decisions are more important than individual ones.

In essence, **individualistic cultures** tend to focus on personal goals whilst **collectivist cultures** expect their members to subordinate personal interests to those of the group.

This divide is rather simplistic; for example, Mediterranean rural societies of Greece and Italy are collectivist within the family but individualistic outside it. Nevertheless, this distinction between cultures is helpful in look-

> **KEY TERMS**
>
> **Individualistic culture** A society in which people focus on personal goals, personal autonomy and individual achievement.
>
> **Collectivist culture** A society based loyalty to the group, interdependence and the belief that individual interests should be subordinated to those of the group.

ing at cultural differences in interpersonal relationships generally and, as we are doing in this chapter, the organisation of marriage.

The two major differences between how marriage partners are selected are, firstly, the degree of choice the couple have in their future spouse and secondly, the extent to which love is seen as a prerequisite to marriage. Fundamental to these differences is the view that in individualistic societies, marriage is a means of fulfilling personal desires and uniting individuals, whilst in collectivist cultures marriage is a vehicle for maintaining social order and uniting families.

Let's first consider the issue of choice. In most traditional collectivist societies the amount of freedom given to youngsters selecting their future spouse is limited. Because of the importance in these cultures of the functioning of the group and of group cohesion, marriages are **arranged**, either by family members or by matchmakers. Nevertheless, the common stereotype that arranged marriages involve no choice by youngsters in who they marry is a myth; in the vast majority of cultures the views of both boy and girl are sought before wedding plans proceed. In Egypt, for example, two sets of parents plan a meeting between children they deem to be suitable matches and only if the pair like each other do they proceed with marriage plans. Since many readers will have an exclusively Western view of arranged marriages, let us take a look at the comments of a writer who in 1977, when he considered himself to be a 'typical sixties London kid', went to Pakistan for an arranged marriage. Strongly supporting the practice, he debunks a common misconception:

> One of the first things that one has to appreciate about arranged marriages is that they have nothing to do with force. Forced mar-

riages are just that – forced. They are common in tribal parts of India, Pakistan and Bangladesh and, in Britain, among sub-continental people from this background … they have little to do with arranged marriages. Arranged marriages are on a different plane: they involve negotiations between mutually consenting, concerned and caring people and are a great source of happiness – both before and after the event of marriage.

(Sardar 1999, p. 16)

On the same theme, in 2008 he writes:

… arranged marriage is a social act because it is not personal and individual. It never involves just two people, each alone with their own angst and dreams. Marriage is much too important to be left to so precarious and potentially perverse and headstrong a basis as the dreams and delusions of a would-be bride and groom. Arranged marriage is not just a marriage between two individuals, but two families.

(Sardar 2008)

DISCUSS AND DEBATE

'I have always been married. My mother harboured a specific plan for my marriage before I was even born. I was married generations before my birth, just as my wife, Saliha, was destined to be my companion before we ever met. We met but briefly and never alone before we were married. As it was, so it is and ever will be, because it works' (Sardar 2008).

This is the first paragraph of the article written by Sardar (2008) for *The Guardian* newspaper. Read the whole article and consider the pros and cons of arranged marriage (available from http://www.guardian.co.uk/lifeandstyle/2008/sep/13/family1).

Would you like your own marriage to be arranged? If so, or if not, why?

So what about love? In the Western world, we tend to take for granted that the basis for a happy marriage is 'being in love'. Simpson *et al.* (1986) found that the vast majority of both men and women in the US view romantic love as a prerequisite to marriage and believe that this plays a crucial role in the maintenance of marriage. However, even if love is not a prerequisite for arranged marriages, this does not mean that it plays no part in them or is not considered important. There is evidence that people in such marriages can eventually be more 'in love' than those who have made their own choices based on romantic love. Gupta and Singh (1982) compared 25 'love' marriages with 25 arranged ones in India, of varying durations. They found that the longer the arranged marriage couples had been married, the higher they scored on Rubin's love scale while the opposite was true of the 'love' marriages. Whereas love was much higher for the 'love' marriages than the arranged ones for comparative newlyweds, for those married ten years or more there was a far higher score on those in the arranged marriages.

In cultures where marriages are not arranged but are heavily influenced by parents (such as orthodox Jews), romantic love is again irrelevant if it would involve marriage outside the religious or ethnic group. In other words, in these cultures, romantic love is taken seriously only as long as it is directed towards a member of one's own group.

It's worth taking a short and interesting digression here to ask whether 'falling in love' is a cultural and historical universal, regardless of its suitability as the basis for marriage. The answer appears to be 'yes'. Despite the contentions of some (e.g. Doi 1963, 1973; Hsu 1985) that passionate love is a Western phenomenon, almost unknown in some cultures such as China and Japan, recent evidence indicates otherwise. Anthropologists now believe that romantic love is a universal characteristic: Jankowiak and Fischer (1992) found evidence of it in 147 out of 166 tribal cultures and in only one were they unable to find any evidence at all of its occurrence. Likewise, historians argue that passionate love has always existed, in all times, in all places. As Hatfield and Rapson (2002, p. 308) comment: 'The earliest Western literature abounds in stories of lovers, fictional and real, caught up in a sea of passion and violence ...'.

In contrast, its suitability as the basis for marriage is anything but universal. In many cultures, including older Western ones, romantic love was not encouraged and it, together with sexual desire, was seen as a threat to social order. In Europe, for example, it was not until the eighteenth century that it was entertained as a consideration in choosing a spouse (Hsu 1971; Murstein 1974).

It is a very different story nowadays. Levine et al. (1995) compared attitudes to love and marriage in 11 different countries (India, Pakistan, Thailand, Mexico, Brazil, Japan, Hong Kong, Republic of the Philippines, Australia, the UK and the US). Using undergraduate participants, they assessed their attitudes to whether romantic love was a prerequisite for marriage and whether its cessation would be adequate grounds for separation or divorce (see page 27 for the questions used). In the US, Brazil,

Australia and the UK, only a tiny percentage of young people said they would consent to marriage without love; in Japan, Hong Kong and Mexico the percentage was slightly higher but love was still seen as a prerequisite to marriage by the majority. Only in collectivist, poorer nations sampled, the Philippines, Thailand, India and Pakistan, did the majority say they would marry someone they did not love if the family saw them as suitable. As this and other research demonstrates, recent times have seen a considerable attitude change with respect to the importance of love as a basis for marriage. Increasingly, youngsters from traditional societies are expressing the wish to have greater personal choice in the selection of a spouse and wish this selection to be on the basis of love (Lieberman & Hatfield 2006). For example, the proportion of arranged marriages in Japan was only 6.4 per cent in 2005, whereas it had been as high as 70 per cent in the early 1940s and 23 per cent in 1988. (Farrer *et al.* 2008). Similar trends are apparent in China, Nepal (Ghimire *et al.* 2006) and other traditional societies. There appears to be a noticeable shift towards greater freedom of choice and an emphasis on love as the basis for marriage in many cultures around the world.

Is there a difference in how various cultures assess the success of a marriage? Another cross-cultural variation in interpersonal relationships is that *psychological intimacy* is more likely to be used as the basis on which to judge marital happiness and personal satisfaction in individualistic societies than in collectivist societies. In the US (and most of the Western world), people view marriage as providing the opportunity to experience personal growth through the relationship and thereby achieve self-fulfilment (Dion & Dion 1993). This can result in very unrealistic expectations and a lack of appreciation of how difficult marriage can be – a rather naïve belief that 'love conquers all' (Heine & Lehman 1995).

Dion and Dion (1993) argue that some aspects of being socialised in an individualistic society make it very difficult to sustain a satisfactory marriage. Western culture, with its emphasis on the importance of independence, personal control and autonomy, makes it very difficult to maintain intimacy even though this is seen as the major goal of a successful marriage. Dion and Dion suggest that this may account for the high divorce rate in the US and Canada. In contrast, collectivist societies place great value on dependency on others and this is therefore a highly valued aspect of close relationships.

Changes in the nature of marriage

One of the most noticeable trends over the last 40 years has been in a decline in marriage around the world. In the US, for example, there was a decline of more than 50% in the annual number of marriages per 1,000 people between 1970 and 2010 (US Census Bureau 2012). The Office of National Statistics (2012) reports that the 'overriding trend' since 1970 has been a decline in both the number of marriages and in marriage rates.

Alongside the decline in marriage, the age at which people marry has increased. In the US in 1958 the average age at which women married for the first time was 20 years and for men it was 23 years. By 1998 it was 25 years for women and 27 years for men. In England and Wales the mean age of first marriage increased by almost 8 years for both men and women between 1970 and 2010, from 24.4 to 32.1 years for men and 22.4 to 30 for women.

The type of ceremony that couples choose when getting married has also changed with a decline in religious ceremonies and an increase in civil ones. Since 1992 the proportion of civil ceremonies has exceeded religious ceremonies in England and Wales; in 2010 less than a third of these ceremonies were religious. The US keeps no nationwide statistics on this, but there is an indication that religious marriage ceremonies there are also on the decline.

The number of times people marry has increased enormously over the years. In England and Wales in 1940, 91 per cent of all marriages were between couples neither of whom had previously been married; by 2010 this figure had dropped to 66 per cent. At the same time, divorce rates have increased: for example, in England and Wales, 22 per cent of marriages in 1970 had ended in divorce by the 15th wedding anniversary, whereas 33 per cent of marriages in 1995 had ended after the same period of time. (However, there is some evidence that the proportion of marriages ending in divorce has levelled off in the very recent years).

One of the most prominent social trends of recent times is the huge increase in the number of couples who live together but are not married. In the US the number of unmarried cohabitees increased 14-fold between 1970 and 2010. In England and Wales, there has been a similar trend: fewer than 1 per cent of adults under 50 are estimated to have cohabitated in the 1960s compared to nearly over 16 per cent by 2010. Alongside this increase goes a considerable attitude change: most people now consider that there is little if any difference socially between being married and cohabiting (Beaujouan & Bhrolcháin, 2011).

Homosexual relationships

Like their heterosexual counterparts, many lesbians and gay men want to commit early and monogamously (McWhirter & Mattison

1984; Lever 1994, 1995). They are strongly in favour of affirming their partnership with ceremonies, celebrations and other symbolic events. The ability to legalise a same-sex union is of profound importance: it acts as a rite of passage, a signal that the relationship is truly committed. It is a means by which the couple can attempt to ensure that their relationship is taken seriously within the family and it also provides legal protection such as rights over children and the right to have a say in the care of an ill and/or dying partner. But whilst legal rights and equality are important, when asked why they had chosen to enter into this ceremony, love, commitment and respect from wider family featured just as strongly in people's accounts (Shipman & Smart 2007).

The issue of legalising same-sex unions is a contentious one and the subject of hot debate. The two main forms of legalisation of a same-sex union are marriage or civil partnership (CP). Same-sex marriage is legal in several countries, including Canada, South Africa, the Netherlands, Norway and Spain. Other countries, such as the UK, France, Germany, and New Zealand, allow civil partnership. (At the time of writing there is a hotly contested bill going through the British parliament to allow 'gay marriage'.) In France and New Zealand, CP is also permitted for heterosexual couples but this is not the case in the UK. The federal government of the US does not recognise same-sex marriages because it defines the concept of marriage as a union between one man and one woman. A small number of States recognise some form of same-sex civil union or marriage but those same-sex couples who have entered into marriage or a civil union still do not qualify for spousal benefits that are established by federal laws and regulations, including tax advantages that married heterosexual couples enjoy.

Some activists argue that, although a civil partnership offers virtually all the rights and benefits of civil marriage, it is discriminatory because there is one law for heterosexuals and another for gays (e.g. Kitzinger & Wilkinson 2004; Tatchell 2005). Wilkinson and Kitzinger (2006, p. 56) state that

> Whatever we think of marriage, access to it is a fundamental issue of equality. As long as marriage is open only to heterosexuals, and civil partnerships only to lesbians and gay men, the British Government is maintaining a symbolic separation of straights and gays, and sending out the clear message that our relationships are of less value to society than heterosexual ones. This is insulting, demeaning, and profoundly discriminatory: an affront to social justice and human rights.

Figure 7.1 Marriage is universal and controlled by many social norms.

There are many commonalities between same-sex and heterosexual couples and, despite some differences, Kurdek (2004, 2005, 2006) argues that the factors predicting relationship satisfaction, commitment and stability are remarkably similar. Regardless of sexuality, most people value affection and dependability and the relationship is more satisfying if the couple share interests, attitudes, values and have a similar level of commitment (Kurdek & Schmitt 1987; Peplau & Fingerhut 2007). In addition, consistent with social exchange theory (see Chapter 4), same-sex relationships are happiest when costs are low and rewards are high. The negotiation involved in trying to resolve conflicts also appears to be similar. Kurdek (1998) found no difference in the frequency of using positive problem-solving styles such as negotiation and compromise or indeed negative ones such as verbal attacks and refusing to talk to the partner. In terms of relationship satisfaction and expressions of love, studies of matched samples of couples reveal no significant differences between same-sex and heterosexual couples (Peplau & Cochran 1980; Kurdek 1998); all couples show a decline in satisfaction over the first few years.

The issue of sexual activity has always been a focus of interest, especially with respect to gay males. Firstly, it is important to note that in all couples, regardless of sexuality, there is a huge variation in sexual frequency. In the early stages of a relationship, gay male couples report having sex more often than do other couples and research consistently finds that lesbian couples have sex less often than either heterosexual or gay male couples (Peplau *et al.* 2004). In terms of the importance of sexual exclusiveness, this is one area in which there are large reported differences between people of different sexual orientations. Gay males put far less emphasis on the importance of monogamy than do lesbian or heterosexual males and females and this is reflected in actual behaviour, with gay men engaging in far more sexual activity outside the relationship and having more sexual partners than other individuals. Relationship satisfaction appears to be positively related to sexual fidelity for lesbian and heterosexual couples but not for gay male couples (Kurdek 1991).

Same-sex couples place great emphasis on equality in relationships and this is reflected in their behaviour. Unlike heterosexual couples who tend to function best when one is dominant and the other submissive, this does not appear to be the case for lesbian couples (Markey & Markey 2011). There is also a more equitable sharing of household tasks among same-sex cohabitees than among heterosexual ones (Kurdek 1993, 2006). In homosexual relationships the allocation of duties, especially household chores, is not taken for granted as in most heterosexual relationships, but is likely to be negotiated. As a result, power struggles are less frequent and dramatic in homosexual relationships than they are in heterosexual ones and underlying resentments about inequality do not have the same opportunity to fester (Peplau *et al.* 1978).

There are also some differences between same-sex and different-sex couples in the way in which they feel about relationship breakup. Gay men and lesbians are more likely than heterosexual couples to stay in touch with partners and maintain a friendship after the relationship has broken up and, whilst in the relationship, to fear the loss of friendship should it end (Harkless & Fowers 2005).

Although the situation in the twenty-first century is certainly better than before same-sex partnerships became legally recognised, prejudice and discrimination is still a problem for lesbians and gay men. In a national survey in the USA (Kaiser Family Foundation 2001), 74 per cent of gay men and lesbians reported experiencing some discrimination based on sexual orientation and a third of them had been rejected by their own families because of it. Overall, many studies show that they receive far less social support from their families than do their heterosexual counterparts (Kurdek 2004, 2006).

Research on same-sex couples is still very limited because, until fairly recently, data from large and representative samples has been difficult to obtain. There are few public records on same-sex relationship formation or breakdown – no marriage or divorce statistics spanning many years – as there are for heterosexual relationships. Research has yet to go beyond the division of household duties and relationship satisfaction and look at issues such as raising children or the mechanisms underlying relationship functioning (Peplau & Fingerhut 2007). Nevertheless, there are indications that this research is underway, especially now that same-sex partnerships are becoming increasingly visible and public policies concerning same-sex marriage and gay adoption are widely discussed.

Summary

- Romantic relationships differ in significant ways from other close relationships, particularly in emotional intensity and in swings of emotion.
- Marriage is universal and controlled by many social norms. There are many mating/marriage systems around the world. Polygyny is permitted in over 80% of societies but practiced in relatively few. Polyandry is extremely rare, permitted in fewer than 1% of societies, often due to poverty. Monogamy is the only legal marriage system in the Western world. There is disagreement over whether monogamy or polygyny is the natural mating pattern in humans.
- Individualistic cultures tend to allow individuals to choose their own marriage partners; the basis for this choice is usually love. Collectivistic cultures are more likely to use arranged marriages in which the family members make the first selection of marriage partner (although some choice is usually available); this is done on the basis of social order, the preservation of any land and uniting families.
- Recent trends in marriage and mating arrangements include:

  o A decline in the number of marriages.
  o An increase in the age at which people marry.
  o An increase in divorce rates.
  o An increase in the number of remarriages.
  o An increase in the number of couples who cohabit.

- Homosexual relationships can be legalised by civil partnership (CP) or by marriage; there are considerable differences in what countries permit. The issue of same-sex marriage is contentious, especially in the UK and the US.

Homosexual and heterosexual relationships are similar in many ways: they both operate in a manner consistent with social exchange theory (SET) and tend to a decline in satisfaction over the first few years. There are also differences. Homosexual relationships tend to be have a more equitable sharing of household tasks than heterosexual ones and a greater emphasis on equality in general. Discrimination and prejudice based on sexual orientation is still a problem for many homosexuals. The lack of long-term data on homosexual relationships makes it difficult to research important issues such as the mechanisms underlying homosexual relationship functioning.

FURTHER READING

Fisher, H. (1992) *The Anatomy of Love: A Natural History of Mating, Marriage, and Why We Stray* (Chapter 3). New York: Fawcett Columbine. [A wonderful book written in a lively style and fascinating.]

Sardar, Z. (2008) First Person. *The Guardian.* 13 September 2008. Available from http://www.guardian.co.uk/lifeandstyle/2008/sep/13/family1

The development of relationships

8

What this chapter will teach you

- How filter theories explain the formation of relationships.

- How Levinger's stage theory explains the way in which relationships change in terms of intimacy.

- How Social Penetration Theory and the Interpersonal Process Models of Intimacy describe the development of relationships.

Stage models of relationship development

When you think about all your own relationships – those with family members, friends, lover, work colleagues – it's not difficult to appreciate that these relationships show changes over time: they are dynamic, not static. In this chapter we consider, first, the way in which we choose certain people rather than others with whom to have a relationship and the processes that relationships pass through as they become more intimate. We then go on to see what behaviours are used to maintain and sustain relationships once they are established. Finally, we consider the effects of relationships on our health and well-being.

Filter and stage models

The first two theories we look at are known as *filter theories* because they are concerned with how, in the early stages of romantic relationships, we successively narrow down our choices until we find a suitable partner. (These theories can also be applied to friendship but their main focus is how we choose our spouses or other life partners). We will then move on to consider a *stage theory* that looks at the life-cycle of intimate relationships.

Kerckhoff and Davis: Filter theory

Kerckhoff and Davis (1962) propose that during courtship people successively narrow down or 'filter out' those with whom they feel they would like to become more intimately involved. At the beginning and end of a seven-month longitudinal study, Kerckhoff and Davis asked student participants in dating relationships to complete questionnaires concerned with family values and the degree to which their own and their partner's needs were complementary, e.g. dominant/submissive. In the second part of the study, the courting couples were also asked to estimate the progress of their relationship by saying whether, compared to seven months before, they thought the likelihood of their forming a permanent relationship was stronger, weaker or unchanged.

Based on the results of this study, Kerckhoff and Davis concluded that filtering takes place in the following sequence:

- The first filter is that of *similarity of social variables* such as class, religion and education. People prefer others who are similar to themselves in these attributes and filter out those who are very different from them. To some extent social circumstances mean that people only come into contact with similar others in terms of ethnicity, race, religion, social class and educational attainment so the 'field of availables' as Kerckhoff calls it, is fairly circumscribed.
- The second filter is that of *agreement on basic values*. This factor has been found to be the most important predicator of a relationship becoming stable and permanent. As with the first filter, those who are very different in their attitudes and values are not considered suitable for a long-term relationship.
- The third filter is that of *complementarity of emotional needs*. People like to be with those whose personality traits are compatible with theirs; complementary behaviours take account of each other's needs and if this occurs then the relationship is likely to become long term.

To summarise, this filter model states that, in the first stage of courtship, similarity of opinions and attitudes is the operative filter and, in the later stages (after about eighteen months), psychological compatibility becomes the decisive factor. In these later stages, social factors have no influence, presumably because most of the partnerships in which values were incompatible have already been filtered out.

This theory has been criticised on several levels, probably the most crucial one being that several researchers have questioned whether we choose partners on the basis of complementary needs. As noted in Chapter 3, although the notion that opposites attract seems plausible, it has not been generally supported by research evidence (e.g. O'Leary & Smith 1991). Indeed, people are more likely to marry others whose needs and personalities are similar, than those who are very different (Berscheid & Reis 1998). Felmlee (1998), in an analysis of 'fatal attractions', found that even when couples were attracted initially by characteristics very different from their own, eventually this could lead to the breakdown of the relationship (see Reflective Exercise 8.1).

There have also been problems with replicating the findings (e.g. Levinger *et al.* 1970), and the model is based on a student-dating population over only 7 months, and so it may not tell us much about the eventual choice of marriage/long-term partner over a longer period or within other populations.

DISCUSS AND DEBATE

What is a 'fatal attraction'?

Most people, when they hear the term 'fatal attraction' immediately think of the classic film, obsession and 'bunny boiling'. In the world of everyday relationships, the type of situation described by the psychologist Felmlee is far less dramatic but no less fatal.

After talking to a large group of participants about their experience of relationship breakdown, Felmlee concluded that there are occasions on which the very characteristics that drew you to a relationship can be responsible for its failure. Felmlee hypothesised that there are three main instances of these:

1 *Fun to foolish* (the most common) – Attracted to their happy-go-lucky outlook and the great fun they are to be with, their behaviour eventually becomes tedious, even humiliating and you now see them as downright immature.
2 *Strong to domineering* – Attracted initially to their self-confident demeanour and strong opinions, you gradually feel that they are too dictatorial, forceful and authoritarian.
3 *Spontaneous to unpredictable* – Drawn to their spontaneity, you gradually find their unpredictable behaviour very unsettling.

Does any of this ring true? Does it support the argument that similarity is attractive whilst dissimilarity leads to uncertainty, a feeling we don't like to have. Discuss!

Murstein: stimulus-value-role (SVR) model

Murstein (1970, 1976) offered an alternative filter theory known as the **stimulus-value-role model**. As in the previous model, this one suggests that the selection of an intimate partner occurs in three stages – at each of which certain options are filtered out and decisions made to maintain, deepen or end the relationship.

1   In the *stimulus stage* we assess the other person in terms of *physical attributes*. If either person fails to provide sufficient reinforcement, no more contact is sought. In everyday language, we decide whether or not we think someone is attractive, and if we do not 'fancy' them we make no overtures that could lead to romantic entanglements. People are generally attracted to those who are similar in age, appearance and ethnicity. At the stimulus stage, no interaction between the couple is required in order for the filtering to take place.

2   In the *value stage* we assess whether or not we have compatible values and attitudes. Particularly important are similarity in attitudes towards family life, religion, career, sex and the role of men and women in society. This stage requires at least verbal interaction and this, in turn, allows each party to examine more closely some of the stimulus variables, such as physical attractiveness and the ability to relate to others. Some couples will marry on the basis of stimulus and value similarity, but for most people this is not enough: if they are compatible so far, they move to the third stage.

3   During the *role stage* partners increasingly confide in each other and become aware of what they desire in a long-term partner and whether or not there is a role 'fit'. Roles themselves may be complementary (you sweep the chimney, I'll feed the rabbit) but *attitudes* towards roles need to be similar in order for the relationship to be harmonious.

Although these stages are relatively distinct, Murstein (1987) pointed out that each of these sets of factors – physical stimuli, values, roles – has *some* influence throughout the courtship, but each one is said to be of paramount importance during only one stage.

Stephen (1985) has criticised Murstein's model on the basis that, like similar models, it portrays matching as a process that occurs via mutual selection rather than something that is achieved through communication. Where opinions differ (rather than end the relationship), a couple may discuss, argue and influence each other until they become compatible. Simply establishing that this similarity of attitudes exists now between a dating couple does not tell us whether or not they have *always* been similar in that respect. Although Murstein disputes this, Stephen convincingly argues that SVR theory sees values, attitudes and beliefs as static (unchanging) characteristics rather than entities that are created or altered by interpersonal communication.

Levinger: Stage theory model

Unlike the previous two models, Levinger's model does not discuss the processes by which we choose a partner but looks at the alterations that take place as a relationship changes in levels of intimacy. It embraces many types of relationship, such as friendship, which may be intimate but not necessarily romantic.

Levinger proposes five possible stages in the development of a close relationship:

A – acquaintance (attraction)
B – buildup
C – continuation (consolidation)
D – deterioration (decline)
E – ending

A – acquaintance

A relationship begins when people are mutually attracted and, as we have already seen, attraction depends largely on similarity in terms of age, social class and so on. A strong source of attraction at the beginning of a romantic relationship is erotic, passionate love. In certain relationships (for example, one between people who work together) the acquaintance stage may last indefinitely.

B – buildup

Buildup involves increasing interdependence. During this stage, the couple engage in increasing amounts of self-disclosure and there is a considerable amount of social exchange, both of pleasure and unpleasantness. Close relationships involve negative aspects, such as disputes and irritating habits, and rewarding ones such as affection and exchange of gifts.

C – continuation

The social norms having been established, the relationship may enter the continuation stage during which it becomes consolidated, and a commitment – such as marriage – may be made. In very long-term relationships the partners enmesh their lives and have many close ties. This stage differs from all the others in that it does not usually involve great intensity of emotion such as elation or rage. It is possible that once a relationship enters into a stable state the partners begin to take each other for granted. The underlying emotional depth of the relationship may not become apparent unless it is threatened. The continuation stage may last indefinitely or the relationship may go downhill.

D – deterioration

Relationships do not necessarily reach the deterioration stage but a large number do. Levinger (1976) used social exchange theory (discussed in Chapter 4) to predict whether a relationship will deteriorate using factors such as costs, rewards, alternatives and barriers to breakdown. He did, however, acknowledge that sometimes breakdown is related to external events or factors.

E – ending

If costs increase, rewards decrease, if attractive alternatives are available and if the barriers to break up are not too high, deterioration is liable to lead to the last stage: the end.

Levinger noted that few relationships actually pass through all five stages. Many never get beyond acquaintance and most terminate at buildup, as one would expect in the majority of friendships.

One major problem with stage theories (and that includes filter theories) is that they portray a situation in which all relationships follow the same linear course in the same direction. However, both the stages themselves and their sequence may not be universal. A number of investigators suggest that the evidence for a fixed sequence of stages is not very convincing. (e.g. Leigh *et al.* 1987). Surra and Huston (1987) asked newly-wed couples how their relationship had developed and discovered a wide variety of sequences. Brehm (1992) comments that, in light of this, rather than use the term 'stages', it is better to view the course of relationships as 'phases' that take place at different times for different couples.

Miell and Crogham (1996) have pointed out several other shortcomings with stage theories. First, they tend to portray a relationship where one active person makes selection decisions involving a passive partner. In reality, a relationship consists of two active people having discussions, making decisions and influencing each other. One example of such mutual influence is that we tend to form friendships only with people who like us and not with those who dislike us. Far from being passive, the actions of the other party have an impact on our reaction and on whether or not we wish to take the relationship any further. And of course this is reciprocal.

Second, there is such a huge diversity in types of relationships (especially friendships) that the generalisations made in these models may not accurately reflect the wide diversity in relationship development.

Third, the experimental procedures involved in research on which these theories are based involve people being presented with artificial tasks, usually the completion of long questionnaires that reveal very little about the complexity of real-life relationships.

With regard to filter theories in particular, Duck (1992) argues that they over-emphasise the role of thought in the selection process while ignoring the extent to which other processes, such as daily interactions, influence our feelings for other people. Whereas we may admire someone for their physical attractiveness and agree with their attitudes and values, they may irritate us intensely when they chatter non-stop at the breakfast table, never put the milk back in the fridge and moan that you leave the lights on (when, as far as you're concerned, they do it just as often).

Despite the fact that stage theories offered a useful framework within which the complexity of real relationships could be explored, the fact that they perhaps offer a view of relationships as considerably more fixed, linear and predictable than they really are, means that they have largely been superseded by process models of relationships. It is to these we will now turn our attention.

Figure 8.1 Sometimes it's not the big issues that cause friction in a relationship but the more mundane ones! © iStock.

Process models of relationship development

Social penetration theory

One of the most important processes in the formation of a close relationship is that of **self-disclosure**, the revealing of private and personal information about yourself that could not, as far as you are concerned, be acquired otherwise.

Self-disclosure is a *gradual* process: people do not usually reveal their innermost thoughts and feelings at a first encounter. It is also a *mutual* process: both parties exchange intimate facts and feelings to each other; if one holds back, the disclosures cease.

Altman and Taylor (1973) discuss this process of self-disclosure in their **social penetration theory**, so-called because it considers the ways in which, as relationships grow increasingly more intimate, they penetrate more and more deeply into the private, social and mental life of the self. The general trend as a relationship develops is for self-disclosures to become less superficial and more intimate; that is, they increase in *breadth* by covering more areas, and in *depth* by covering more and more sensitive and important topics.

Altman and Taylor describe the following changes that occur in the types of exchange as a relationship becomes more intimate.

In the *orientation stage* we engage in a lot of 'small talk' and use noncontroversial clichés ('it takes all sorts', 'practice makes perfect'). Then follows the *exploratory affective* stage in which we express personal attitudes ('I'm not keen on Christmas myself, it's a bit too commercialised now: OK for the kids though') but avoid intimate ones. In the early stages of self-disclosure we do not tell the whole truth and nothing but the truth: we provide limited and even false information about ourselves in order to give a favourable impression. Many interpersonal relationships never get beyond the exploratory affective exchanges, but others do move on to the *affective stage*, during which we now begin to discuss very personal and private matters, and this level of self-disclosure is accompanied by physical affection. Friends, especially female friends, may touch affectionately, lovers will kiss and touch intimately. Very close relationships will eventually reach the stage of *stable exchange* in which all personal feelings and possessions are shared and each can readily predict the feelings and behaviour of the other.

As mentioned above, the process of self-disclosure is a mutual one in which any exchanges made by one person must be matched by the other or the relationship will not deepen. This matching process is especially important in the early stages of a relationship, but later on, strict reciprocity is not necessary, as the relationship is sufficiently well established not to require it.

The increase in intimacy is not necessarily a smooth and gradual one. Many relationships follow a more variable, cyclical pattern of self-disclosure (Altman *et al.* 1981; Derlega *et al.* 1993). Some pairs mutually self-disclose very quickly, then stop quite abruptly; others show a quick start and then a plateau, while others show a steady rise followed by a lull or a decline.

When relationships that were intimate begin to break down, self-disclosures often narrow to a very few acrimonious topic areas, but they are still deeply penetrating as partners bombard each other with hurtful insults and recriminations (Tolstedt and Stokes 1984).

The importance of self-disclosure in any relationship should not be underestimated. When we share intimate information about ourselves to others, we are showing that we trust them not to violate our confidences and that we are committed to the relationship. By such revelations, we are inviting them to make their own disclosures and thereby to enter into a close and mutually supportive relationship with us.

The interpersonal process model of intimacy

The previous model emphasises the importance of self-disclosure in a relationship. The interpersonal process model of intimacy (Reis & Shaver 1988; Reis & Patrick 1996) does not underestimate the importance of self-disclosure but argues that it does not entirely capture the phenomenon of intimacy, which is an essential component of a relationship. There is a variety of definitions of intimacy but the one thing they have in common is a feeling of closeness and connectedness that develops through communication between partners (Perlman & Fehr 1987).

The interpersonal process model of intimacy sees self-disclosure as the first step to intimacy: a relationship is initiated when one person communicates personally relevant and revealing information, thoughts and feelings to another person. These communications can be nonverbal as well as verbal: leaning forward, a gentle touch, making eye-contact. These nonverbal communications may amplify the verbal ones or stand alone as a means of self-disclosure (Keeley & Hart 1994). The model distinguishes between types of such disclosures – some are more related to intimacy than are others. So-called **emotional or evaluative disclosures** (ones that express personal feelings) are more closely related to intimacy than are *factual or descriptive* disclosures (information about yourself). Emotional disclosures allow more core aspects of yourself to be known thereby facilitating the meeting of your interpersonal needs.

For the intimacy process to continue, there must be an appropriate response from the partner, one that captures the content of the communication, demonstrates concern for the discloser, is sincere and immediate, and meets the needs of the discloser (Berg 1987). In essence it must convey acceptance, validation and caring for the individual who has made the disclosure. However, for intimacy to develop it is not sufficient for the responder to show these qualities in their response but for the individual who made the disclosure to interpret it in this way: he or she must *feel* understood, validated and cared for. The roles of speaker and listener in this process are dynamic and fluid. As each partner's self becomes known and validated by the other, the experience of mutual intimacy is increased.

The perceptions that partners have of each other's disclosures can be influenced by a number of individual differences (personality traits). Davis (1982) suggests several dispositional factors that may influence the depth of intimacy that a relationship reaches. These include:

- *Self-monitoring*: the extent to which people are aware of social cues and situational factors and adapt their behaviour accordingly. High **self-monitors** are more attentive and respond more appropriately than low self-monitors (Shaffer *et al.* 1982).
- *Communication accuracy*: the ability to understand communication is related to extraversion, self-consciousness and self-monitoring; the ability to make an appropriate response is related to intelligence, memory and interpersonal skills.
- *Motivation to maintain responsiveness*: people differ in the extent to which they care about being responsive to others. Those high in intimacy motivation and extraversion will be more responsive than those who are low in this motivation.

This process model of intimacy conceptualises intimacy as a dynamic process unfolding over time and emphasises the argument that relationships are processes, not states. It also allows for the fact that intimacy itself is not a static state within any particular relationship but varies even on day-to-day basis.

There is considerable research evidence in support of this model. Lin (1992) and Laurenceau *et al.* (1998) both found disclosure of emotion was more important in the development of intimacy than was factual self-disclosure. Laurenceau *et al.* (1998) also found evidence for the conceptualisation of intimacy as a combination of self-disclosure and partner responsiveness. Lippert and Prager (2001), using a sample of romantic, cohabiting couples who completed interaction diaries assessing intimacy, found feelings of intimacy were positively related to both disclosures and perception of partner responsiveness. Laurenceau *et al.* (2005) looked at intimacy in the daily lives of married couples and found validity for the model. Based on daily diary accounts of interactions over 42 days, they found that self-disclosure and partner disclosure appreciably contributed to the prediction overall of relationship intimacy. These findings are particularly significant given that they reflect on-going daily marital interactions rather than those in short-term dating relationships.

This model has important practical implications in the field of relationship satisfaction and counselling. Given that intimacy is essential to a well-functioning long-term relationship and that its absence indicates dysfunction (Fruzzetti 1996),

RESEARCH QUESTIONS

Both Lippert and Prager (2001) and Laurenceau *et al.* (2005) used the diary method to collect data on intimacy. Discuss the advantages and disadvantages of the diary method of collecting data.

this model has a great deal to contribute to the understanding of the development of close, satisfying marital relationships and the repair of unsatisfactory ones. Huston *et al.* (2001) suggest that the abatement of intimacy in a relationship is more likely to lead to divorce than is conflict between the partners. This model acknowledges that a sense of responsiveness by each partner (understanding, acceptance, validation and caring) in addition to self-disclosure is an essential component of a satisfying, loving relationship.

Summary

- Kerckhoff and Davis's (1962) filter theory proposes that, when choosing a romantic partner, we first choose from people similar to ourselves on social variables. From these we select those with the basic values and from these people, those with complementary emotional needs.

- Murstein's stimulus-value-role (SVR) model proposes that the first filter is those we find physically attractive; the second one is those who have the same values as us and the third one is those people who have the same ideas on the roles within marriage (or other long-term partnership).
- Levinger's stage theory, the ABCDE model, looks at how relationships change in levels of intimacy. The stages are acquaintance, build-up, continuation, deterioration, ending. Relationships can stop at any of these stages and relatively few pass through all five.
- Stage models have been criticised for assuming that all relationships go through the same stages in the same order. Process theories are now considered more relevant.
- Social Penetration Theory (Altman & Taylor 1973) considers the way in which self-disclosure in a relationship leads it to be increasingly more intimate. People move gradually from superficial disclosures (the orientation stage) to disclosures about attitudes (the exploratory stage) on to revelations of a very private nature (the affective stage). Finally they reach the stage of stable exchange in which all personal feelings and possessions are shared.
- The Interpersonal Process Model of Intimacy looks in detail at self-disclosure as a dynamic process between the two parties in which disclosures must be mutually validated in order for the relationship to progress. The perception that each partner has of the other's disclosures depends on individual differences including self-monitoring, communication accuracy, and motivation to maintain responsiveness. Intimacy within a relationship is a process, not a state, and varies even on a day to day basis.

FURTHER READING

Prager, K. (1995) *The Psychology of Intimacy*. New York: Guilford Press.
Regan, P. (2011). *Close Relationships* (Chapter 6). New York: Routledge.

The maintenance and effects of relationships $\quad$ 9

What this chapter will teach you

- The types of maintenance strategies used to sustain relationships.

- How these strategies are used in different relationships.

- Why these strategies are used.

- The effects of close relationships on health and well-being.

Communication in relationships: maintenance strategies

At the start of the previous chapter we said that relationships are not static, they move along. They simply do not work if nothing is done to sustain them; without nourishment they die. In order to sustain well-functioning relationships people use **maintenance strategies**, that is, *behaviours that ensure the continuation of a valued relationship*. These behaviours serve to sustain equilibrium within the relationship and achieve a sufficiently high level of satisfaction to prevent its dissolution.

> **KEY TERM**
>
> **Maintenance strategies** Behaviours that sustain a relationship and ensure its continuation.

Stafford and Canary (1991) produced one of the earliest classifications of such strategies as applied to romantic relationship and, although many other such strategies have been suggested, this classification remains the one used most often by researchers. Stafford and Canary suggest five major types of maintenance behaviour: *positivity*; *openness*; *assurances*; *social networks*; and *sharing tasks.*

Table 9.1 gives a brief description of each of these strategies and an example of the type of comment made by participants when describing various types of relationships (taken from Canary *et al.* 1993).

Table 9.1 Five major types of maintenance behaviour

Maintenance strategy	Description/ subcategories	Example of comment made
Positivity	Attempts to make interactions cheerful and pleasant.	I try to be upbeat and positive about her.
Openness	Direct discussion and listening to another. Includes self-disclosure.	We share things about each other that no-one else knows.
Assurances	Covertly and overtly assuring each other of the importance of the relationship.	We try to put each other first.
Social networks	Relying on the support of friends and family.	We rely on her twin sister to help us with problems
Sharing tasks	Performing routine tasks and chores in a relationship.	We share the cleaning responsibilities.

Source: From Canary *et al.* (1993).

Figure 9.1 Sharing routine tasks is an important maintenance strategy in relationships.
© images.com/Corbis

Although these five strategies remain the classic typology of such behaviours, others have been added.

Canary *et al.* (1993) expanded their research to include other types of relationships, including kinships, friendships and co-workers and added five more strategies: *joint activities*; *cards, letters and calls*; *avoidance*; *anti-social*; and *humour*. The first two speak for themselves (it's worth mentioning that joint activities are very important in relationships). Avoidance involves evasion of partner issues: avoiding certain topics, giving the partner/friend alternative associations and allowing independence. Anti-social strategies are behaviours that seem unfriendly or coercive, e.g. acting in a jealous manner. Humour involves the use of jokes and sarcasm, so can be positive or negative.

RESEARCH ISSUE

Ethics

The work of Canary *et al.* (1993) raises some interesting issues with regard to ethics. As in this case, it is not unusual for research projects to use data collected from the assignments that students complete as an obligatory part of a course. It is therefore essential to ensure that the participants are under no obligation to allow their work to be used in the research. In this particular research, the investigators used information from assignments of students on a course in interpersonal communication. The students were required to write about the type of communication behaviours they used in three different relationships and the information from these was coded by two different trained coders.

The following ethical considerations were made:

- Participation in the research was entirely voluntary and solicited after the assignment was completed.
- It was made clear that the grades awarded for the assignment were not at all dependent on participating in the research.
- Confidentiality was assured.
- Written consent was sought for voluntary participation.

Which principles from the APA Ethical Principles of Psychologists and Code of Conduct were the researchers following? (see http://www.apa.org/ethics/code/index.aspx# if you need a copy of these).

Dainton and Stafford (1993) extended the work on romantic relationships by looking at routine behaviours that couples share. These included some of the ones already mentioned, namely joint activities, avoidance, antisocial, plus two more: affection (e.g. touching, kissing and sexual intimacy) and focus on self (e.g. watching one's weight or furthering a career).

In 2000, Stafford et al. added yet another two strategies used in romantic relationships, those of conflict management and advice. Conflict management involves behaviours that reduce instability, such as cooperation or apologising; advice refers to sharing your opinion in support of your partner.

Having identified the main strategies that people use to maintain satisfactory relationships, researchers looked at how these strategies are used.

Canary et al. (1993) showed that maintenance strategies vary according to the type of relationship. Romantic partners and family members appear to use more positivity, openness, assurances, sharing tasks and cards/letters/calls more than friends do. The researchers suggest that this could be because there is greater interdependence in kinships and romantic relationships which therefore require more conscious effort to ensure that the relationships function in the way in which the participants desire. In essence, people are probably less concerned about maintaining their friendships than their romantic and family relationships. Friends can be taken for granted!

Among friends, positivity and networks are used more frequently than other strategies (Nix 1999; Messman et al. 2000).

In romantic relationships, whether heterosexual or homosexual, shared tasks are the most frequently used maintenance behaviours (Dainton & Stafford 1993; Haas & Stafford 1998).

The use of strategies also varies according the particular stage of a relationship. When romantic relationships are 'on the up', then openness and assurances are perceived to increase; when they begin to deteriorate then the use of positivity, assurances and shared tasks start to decrease (Guerrero et al. 1993).

Why do we need to use these strategies to maintain a relationship in a satisfactory state? Explanations have been based on both theories of interpersonal relationships and on individual characteristics of the partners.

One explanation for the reason why these strategies are used is based on equity theory, discussed in Chapter 4. Basically it states that for a relationship to be satisfactory, the amount that each partner puts in to a relationship (costs) must be the same as what they get out of it (benefits). If one person has greater output (benefit) than input, they are said to be over-benefitted. If they get less out than they put in, they are under-benefitted. Canary and Stafford (2001) argue that behavioural maintenance strategies are both inputs and outputs. The behaviour itself (e.g. complimenting partner; being cheerful) is the input (cost) whilst perceiving this behaviour (being complimented; having a cheerful partner) is the output (benefit). Canary and Stafford (1992) found that, as predicted, people in equitable relationships made the greatest use of maintenance strategies whilst under-benefitted individuals used least, presumably because their inputs were already greater than their rewards.

Another approach is to consider the extent of uncertainty in a relationship, which researchers have shown, is negatively related to the use maintenance strategies. Ficara and Mongeau (2000) found that the more uncertain an individual was in a relationship, the less they used assurances, openness and positivity. Dainton and Aylor (2001) found a negative correlation between all five of the original maintenance strategies and uncertainty. Of course, it is likely that inequity and uncertainty are linked: individuals who feel that their relationship is inequitable may well be uncertain about the relationship, especially if they are under-benefitted.

What interests researchers is the reason for the correlation between the maintenance behaviours and inequity and uncertainty. Is uncertainty in a relationship *caused* by the lack of maintenance behaviours or does uncertainty *cause* the individual to use fewer maintenance behaviours? Dainton (2011) suggests that the key is the *perception* by an individual as to whether their partner is using relationship maintenance. If, for example, a person has no interest in sharing activities with their partner, rarely or never gives assurance that they love or like them, is not open about their feelings and shows little affection, then the individual feels uncertain about whether their feelings for their partner are reciprocated. In other words, it is the lack of maintenance behaviours that causes the uncertainty. Canary and Stafford's (2001) finding that there is an association between perceptions of a partner's behaviour and inequity (especially under-benefittedness) supports this contention.

It is logical that researchers seeking to explain the use of relational maintenance behaviours in romantic relationships should focus on the dynamics of the relationship itself, often in terms of social exchange theories. However, as the researchers involved fully acknowledge, their attempts have not always met with great success. Some behaviours can indeed be explained in terms of equity, uncertainty and interdependence, but others cannot. As Ragsdale and Brandau-Brown (2005) point out, efforts to predict the use of maintenance strategies from scores on scales such as equity, investment, uncertainty, even quality of alternatives to the relationship, have not been successful. These researchers suggest a complementary approach that looks towards *individual communicator variables* such as self-monitoring and Machiavellianism in search of explanations.

Let's just consider Machiavellianism. Traditionally, maintenance behaviours have been seen as attempts to keep the relationship in a satisfactory state by attending to the partner's needs. However, another purpose may be less altruistic, the need to get your own way, appropriately labelled as Machiavellianism. Ragsdale and Brandau-Brown (2005) found that men who are high in the ability to modify their self-presentation tend to use a great deal of positivity, perhaps as a deliberate attempt to create a good atmosphere in which to get their own way. Men who are attentive to social comparison make a lot of use of network and sharing tasks and women high in cynicism and attentive to social comparison were also likely to network more than others.

This work on individual communicator indicators is in its infancy but may prove fruitful in explaining the use of maintenance strategies. Already, research indicates that attachment style is an important variable in that secure individuals tend to use assurances, affection and openness more than do dismissive individuals; preoccupied individuals make considerable use of assurances and openness while avoidant individuals make little use of affection, openness and social networks (Guerrero & Bachman 2006). The dimension of dogmatism may be another salient individual characteristic worthy of research attention. Ragsdale and Brandau-Brown (2005, p. 72) comment that

> Rather than searching only for interpersonal sources of motivation or variations in the evolution of the relationship, researchers might be able to construct something more like a profile of the relational maintainer. Knowledge that such behaviour might lie in individual differences and in the dynamics of the marital relationship could be of great benefit to teachers of interpersonal and family communication.

Effects of close relationships on health and well-being

For better or worse – in sickness or in health

Throughout this book we have looked at how relationships, or indeed the lack of them, have a profound effect on us, both positive and negative. In this section we will look in more detail at the effects of relationships on our health and well-being.

A multitude of studies testify to the health enhancing properties of good relationships. Statistics from industrialised countries consistently show that the less involvement people have in social relationships in general the more likely they are to die early (e.g. Berkman & Syme 1979; House *et al*. 1988). This difference still exists when other factors, such as socioeconomic status, health behaviour and other variables that might affect longevity are taken into account (e.g. Brummett *et al*. 2001). In some cases the differences are staggeringly large – Brummett *et al*. (2001) found that, amongst adults with coronary heart disease, the risk of death from this condition was 2.4 times greater in the socially isolated than in those who had a good social network.

People who have few good quality close relationships are more susceptible than the well socially connected to a range of illnesses and poor health conditions, including high blood pressure, cancer, cardiovascular disease and slower healing of wounds (Ertel *et al*. 2009; Everson-Rose & Lewis 2005; Robles & Kiecolt-Glaser 2003). Physical health is better for the employed than for the unemployed who have lost relationships with work colleagues (although factors other than relationship loss may be implicated here), and for those with children compared with the childless (Warr 1983). In a series of studies, Kiecolt-Glaser has shown that the immune system is boosted by good social support and adversely affected by lack of social support or poor quality relationships (e.g. Kiecolt-Glaser *et al*. 2002, 2010).

Marriage appears to be associated with particular health advantages. As long ago as 1851, and in many studies since, statistics have indicated that married people live longer than those who are unmarried (Farr 1975; Hu & Goldman 1990; Kaplin & Kronick 2006). Historically, research tended to concentrate on the single, married, widowed or divorced but in an era in which patterns of marriage are very different, researchers are looking increasingly at the health implications for those many individuals who have experienced a disrupted marriage followed by one or more remarriages. Hughes and Waite (2009) investigated the relationship between marital history and several measures of health in a large nationally representative sample of mid-life adults in the USA. They found that on all the health dimensions, currently married people who had never been divorced or widowed showed better health than currently married people with experience of marital loss. The health advantages of the continuously married over the remarried were largest for chronic conditions and smallest for depressive ones. Interestingly, they found little evidence that people who had experienced multiple disruptions were in any worse health than those who had experienced a single disruption. Neither did they find any health advantages in being married for a long time: in the continuously married, those married the longest were no healthier at mid-life than those with shorter marriages; if anything there was a small tendency towards the reverse. One strong difference was between those who had remarried and those who had remained single after a disrupted marriage: in later life the health of the remarried was consistently better than those who had remained unmarried.

Close, harmonious relationships are particularly important for good mental as well as physical health. Women experiencing considerable stress were much less likely to be depressed if they had a supportive spouse with whom to share their problems than if they had no such social support (Brown & Harris 1978; Brown et al. 1986). In contrast, the divorced and separated are more likely than the married to suffer from depression, commit suicide, abuse alcohol and receive treatment for psychiatric disorders (Berkman et al. 2000; Wade & Pevalin 2004).

Wade and Pevalin (2004) took measures of mental health at various times in groups of people who had experienced marital disruption and found that it declined following divorce, separation or widowhood. In those who were separated or divorced there had been a prevalence of mental health problems before the separation and a decline afterwards, indicating that poor mental health may have been both the cause and consequence of the relationship disruption. Perhaps unsurprisingly a different pattern emerged in the widowed in which the lowest point in mental health (especially depression) centred around the time of death with no mental health problems prior to the onset of the circumstances leading to the death of the spouse.

Although close harmonious relationships may have a very positive effect on individuals, discordant ones can be a source of great stress. The presence of a spouse is not necessarily health enhancing if the marriage is unhappy; indeed, unmarried people are happier, on average, than unhappily married people (Glenn 1989) and depression is strongly associated with marital discord (Beach et al. 1998; Fincham & Beach 1999). As Berkman et al. (2000) point out, it is important not to overlook the fact that 'some of the most powerful impacts on health that social relationships may have are through acts of abuse, violence, and trauma' (p. 854).

Some researchers have looked at the effects of social support versus social strain. Walen and Lachman (2000) examined the relationship between social exchanges on the one hand and well-being and health on the other in a sample of married and cohabiting individuals. They assessed the quality of social exchanges by asking the participants to assess, for example, how much their spouse/partner really cared about them. They found that positive and negative exchanges were more strongly related to psychological well-being than to health, although partner strain was still predictive of health problems. The protective effect of a supportive network and the detrimental effects of family strain affected both sexes but the effects were greater in women than in men.

Sadly, stress in relationships can adversely affect health and well-being throughout the lifespan and children are not immune to it. Physiological arousal due to stress can have a cumulative negative affect on health (e.g. high blood pressure, strain on the cardiovascular system) while psychological stress can lead people into damaging behaviours such as smoking, poor eating habits, alcohol or other drug abuse (Kassel *et al.* 2003).

However loving a relationship may be, caring for a sick or injured spouse can be detrimental to both physical and mental health, and to well-being. Research indicates that caring for a loved one can lead to impaired immune functioning and poorer health behaviour (Schulz & Sherwood 2008).

Research from the 1970s and beyond indicated that there were considerable gender differences in the effect of relationships, with men being greater beneficiaries than women. Gove (1972) argued that marriage was beneficial to the mental health of men but deleterious to the mental health of women. Argyle and Henderson (1985) suggestion that men gain more than do women from intimate relationships because women provide more support than do men: they are more affectionate, appreciative, encouraging and more inclined to share intimacy (Argyle & Henderson 1985). Fincham (1997), after surveying a hundred couples, concluded that although marriage is beneficial to the mental health of men, it has the opposite effect in women who are very often depressed within their marriages. These findings may reflect the fact that women, like men, benefit from a supportive relationship but, once things start to go wrong and there is marital disharmony, women are disproportionately more affected than men and become susceptible to depression.

In the decades since this research was published there have been profound social changes in men's and women's roles and in marital patterns. It is therefore not surprising that modern research paints a rather different picture of gender differences in the effects of marriage and cohabiting. Waite and Gallagher (2000) argue that marriage is beneficial to the mental and physical health of both men and women who live longer and healthier lives than their unmarried counterparts. Simon (2002), having carried out longitudinal analyses, argues that it is true that social roles in general and marital roles in particular do have consequences for mental health but that Gove's (1972) findings no longer reflect these consequences. Overall, getting married decreases distress whilst marital loss increases it (although this only applies to certain groups of people and for certain types of emotional problems). Older research was criticised for concentrating on depression, which appears to affect women more than men, whilst ignoring other mental health issues. In his analysis, Simon included men's alcohol problems, which, he believes, are the 'functional equivalent' of women's depression. Once this is taken into account the gender differences on the impact of marital transitions need to be looked at in a different light. In times of stress, such as marital breakdown, women internalise their distress by becoming depressed while men tend to externalise their emotional problems by turning to alcohol. Overall, Simon's (2002) findings indicate that, at least in the USA at the time of writing, marriage is not deleterious to women but has significant benefits for both sexes.

DISCUSS AND DEBATE

The work of Gove (1972), Fincham (1997) and others on the relative benefits of marriage/cohabiting for men and women demonstrates the need to have up-to-date research. However, this does not mean that older research is not important in providing information on the effect of relationships; it does, however, point to the need to put it in an historical context.

Discuss the ways in which married and romantic relationships have changed in the last 50 years (information from Chapter 7 will be useful here) and the effect this has had on health and happiness.

There are two main competing hypotheses as to the reasons why people in marriage are more mentally stable than the separated or divorced. The **social selection hypothesis** postulates that people with mental health problems are less likely to remain married than the mentally stable (mental health problems cause the marriage to deteriorate). The **social causation hypothesis** argues that emotional distress is the result of the marriage breakdown and the factors leading up to it (deterioration of the marriage causes the mental health problems). Although findings from longitudinal research are complex and difficult to interpret, it appears likely that both of these hypotheses are true. Whilst it is likely that depression and alcohol problems may

KEY TERM

Social selection hypothesis People with mental health problems are less likely to remain married than those who are mentally stable (mental health problems cause the marriage breakdown).

Social causation hypothesis Mental health problems are the result of problems within the marriage (stress in the marriage causes the mental health problems).

precipitate a marital breakdown, it is also likely that these problems increase as a consequence of the stress involved in that breakdown. In addition, although it may be a minor factor, we cannot dismiss prosperity as a third factor controlling both better health and better marriage prospects. As Durkin (1995) remarks, rich people are not only very likely to get married because they are a very attractive proposition, but 'the lovely and the loaded tend to live well, and are less exposed to malnutrition, hazardous environments, depression, and other health threats associated with lower social status' (p. 611).

What are the routes by which relationships have an effect on mental and physical health? Berkman et al. (2000) suggest four interrelated means by which networks of relationships have an effect on health, some positive, some negative:

- *Provision of social support*. This can promote health in a variety of ways.
  - *Instrumental support*. Family and friends provide practical support, especially in times of need. They may cook meals, do the shopping and ensure that medicine is taken.
  - *Emotional support*. People who feel supported are less adversely physically affected by stressful events than those who lack support. Cohen and Hoberman (1982) found that, of people who felt their life to be very stressful, those who received little social support suffered more symptoms such as headaches, weight loss and sleep disturbances than those who perceived themselves as having high support. Supportive interactions with others can also have a direct, beneficial physiological effect on the immune, endocrine and cardiovascular systems (Uchino 2004). Nuckolls et al. (1972) compared complication rates in pregnant women who were experiencing different levels of stress. They found that 91 per cent of women with high stress and low social support suffered complications, compared to 33 per cent who also suffered high stress but had high levels of social support.
  - *Informational support*. Social networks, such as self-help groups for the seriously ill, may also provide information that is of practical help. Goleman (1990) found that seriously ill people who joined support groups had more effective immune systems and tended to live longer than those without such support.
- *Social influence*. Other people's attitudes and behaviour can have a profound effect on people especially if they are part of a close network. Peer group pressure can influence people to start

smoking or, indeed, to give it up. Eating behaviours are greatly affected by social norms within friendship groups or internet networks and can result in anorexia, bulimia or over-eating. Conversely, the social norms of a group can also promote a healthy lifestyle in general such as taking regular exercise and healthy eating.

- *Social engagement and attachment*. The feeling of belonging to a group increases self-esteem and security, which in turn gives meaning to life and promotes longevity. In addition, as documented in Bowlby's work (discussed in Chapter 1) early childhood experiences of attachment have a profound effect on the capacity for individuals to develop meaningful relationships in later life and this in turn has implications for healthy emotional and physical development.
- *Access to resources and material goods*. Although not a lot of attention has been paid to this, social networks operate to control people's access to life opportunities, health care, housing and institutional contacts, all of which have an influence on health and well-being.

This model is not the only one to suggest ways in which relationships and health are interrelated but it is one of most comprehensive and takes account of factors other than social support functions. As the authors acknowledge there is certainly yet more work to be done in this field, especially with regard to cross-cultural work comparing countries with different values regarding social relationships, community and sense of obligation. It may also be a time to reflect on the future implications for relationships and health in the Western world in which the tendency towards smaller families, high divorce rates, geographic mobility and other factors such as an ageing population, mean that in the future there is liable to be fewer family ties and more social isolation.

Summary

- Various maintenance strategies serve to sustain relationships. The five basic ones (Stafford & Canary 1991) are positivity, openness, assurances, social networks and sharing tasks.
- Different relationships use different types of maintenance strategy. Friends use fewer maintenance strategies than do family members and romantic partners.

- People in equitable relationships make the greatest use of maintenance strategies and under-benefitted individuals use least.
- The fewer maintenance strategies that are used by one partner, the more the other partner experiences uncertainty about the relationship.
- Relationships have a considerable effect on health and well-being.
  - Married people live longer than their single counterparts.
  - Those who have many social connections are less prone to illnesses or poor health conditions than those less well connected.
  - The immune system is boosted by good social support and adversely affected by a lack of it.
  - People with close harmonious relationships are also more likely to have good mental health than those who lack such relationships. Mental health is likely to deteriorate following divorce, separation and widowhood.
  - Older research indicated that, in terms of mental health, men benefitted from marriage whilst it had a deleterious effect on women. Data from 2000 onwards indicate that marriage and cohabiting is beneficial to both sexes.
  - There are several proposed means by which marriage has an advantageous effect on physical and mental health: provision of social support, social influence, social engagement (a feeling of belonging), and greater access to resources.

FURTHER READING

Canary, D.J., Stafford, L., Hause, K.S. & Wallace, L.A. (1993) An inductive analysis of relational maintenance strategies: Comparisons among lovers, relatives, friends, and others. *Communication Research Reports, 10*, 5–14. [This paper provides examples of maintenance behaviors.]

Duck, S. (2007) *Human Relationships* (4th edn, Chapter 3). Thousand Oaks, CA: Sage.

Morrison, V. & Bennett, P. (2012) *An Introduction to Health Psychology* (3rd edn, Chapter 15). Upper Saddle River, NJ: Pearson Education Ltd.

The deterioration of relationships

10

What this chapter will teach you

- Some statistics on the frequency of divorce.
- The types of conflict that cause dissatisfaction in marriage.
- How attributions (ideas about the cause of behaviour) are related to marital satisfaction.
- The Vulnerability-Stress-Adaptation Model of marriage.
- Rusbult and Zembrodt's model of responses to relationship dissatisfaction.
- Duck's model of the processes involved in marital breakdown.

'… to love and to cherish, till death us do part'. The vast majority of marriages start out with a couple who are very much in love and vow to stay together forever, yet, despite the optimistic belief in a bright and happy future, one in three marriages in Britain breaks down before the 15th anniversary and the average marriage lasts only 11.4 years (Office of National Statistics 2012). In the US about 20 per cent of all first marriages have been disrupted by separation or divorce within 5 years; this figure jumps to 33 per cent after 10 years and 43 per cent after 15 years (Bramlett & Mosher 2002); the rate of dissolution for remarriages is even higher than for first ones (Cherlin 1992).

Even within intact first marriages the reported satisfaction levels have declined steadily since the mid-1970s (National Marriage Project 1999). In addition, contrary to the once-held belief that after a decline in satisfaction, the level gradually increased again following a U-shaped curve (e.g. Rollins & Feldman 1970) more recent research indicates that it drops markedly over the first 10 years and more gradually from then on (Glenn 1998) with no 'bounce back'.

The effects of deteriorating relationships are profound and widespread. The costs are societal as well as individual, so much so that distressed and broken relationships are a matter of public policy. The fallout from them is implicated in many problem areas for society: childhood unhappiness and behavioural problems, drug and alcohol abuse, loneliness, violence, depression, to name but a few.

So what goes wrong? In this chapter we will consider various models that look at the interpersonal processes within marriage and at sociocultural factors that may help explain why serious romantic relationships come to an end (and, indeed, why some remain intact). We will also consider the process through which couples pass when a romantic relationship breaks down.

Conflict within relationships

Conflict occurs in a relationship when the actions of one person interfere with the actions of another (Peterson 1983). We are all familiar with it simply because it is inevitable in interpersonal relationships. Its likelihood increases as two people become more interdependent: the closer the relationship, the more potential there is for conflict. It varies from the comparatively trivial (perhaps!), when two people want to watch TV together but can't agree on a programme, to the more serious, when one partner wants to take a job which requires a house move and the other does not want to go. The latter is probably an unusual conflict but the former is not: everyday life is full of them.

Conflict occurs in all types of relationships. Close friends argue almost every day (Burk & Laursen 2005); pre-school children squabble regularly (Ljungberg et al. 2005) and there cannot possibly be a family, especially one that includes teenagers or, for that matter, any children, in which differences of opinion, arguments and rows are not a common occurrence (Adams & Laursen 2007).

Sources of conflict are manifold: people will argue about almost anything. Kurdek (1994) listed the six most common general issues that cause conflict within intimate relationships, be they gay, homosexual or heterosexual as:

1   Power: e.g. who makes the decisions, who does the majority of housework.
2   Social issues: e.g. personal values, political opinions.
3   Personal flaws: e.g. driving, drinking alcohol, personal hygiene.
4   Distrust: e.g. lying, previous lovers.
5   Intimacy: e.g. sex, lack of affection.
6   Personal distance: e.g. frequent absences, long distance jobs.

The way in which conflicts are dealt with varies greatly from relationship to relationship. Some people will successfully negotiate them and the partners will remain in a harmonious state but other people will react in a manner that leads to dissatisfaction and even breakdown. One model that has been extremely influential in relationship research looks at the explanations provided by individuals for their partner's behaviour and it is to this that we now turn our attention.

Attributions of behaviour in intimate relationships

An important factor that appears to be associated with satisfaction in relationships is the **attributions** or explanations people give to their partner's behaviour. The way in which behaviours, particularly annoying and irritating ones, are interpreted can make a significant difference to whether or not conflicts are successfully resolved. Suppose that in a partnership one person forgets to buy a loaf

> **KEY TERM**
>
> **Attribution of behaviour** The explanation someone gives for behaviour (to what they attribute it). An internal attribution explains the behaviour in terms of the person (she is considerate) and an external attribution explains behaviour in terms of circumstances (he was late because the bus was delayed).

of bread on the way home. This can be interpreted as a minor incidental matter caused by certain circumstances such as having other things on your mind. It can alternatively be attributed to a far more serious, negative aspect of personality, for example, that the miscreant is selfish, inconsiderate and lazy. Likewise, positive behaviours, such as a cuddle or a gift, can be attributed in a negative fashion (he or she is 'after something') or a positive one (he or she is very affectionate).

Attribution theorists propose that there are three dimensions on which we can judge the cause of any behaviour:

- *Locus*: the extent to which the behaviour is rooted in the individual:
  - o an *internal* attribution means that the person is held responsible;
  - o an *external* attribution means that the behaviour is seen as caused by circumstances.
- *Globality*: the extent to which the behaviour affects other parts of the relationship:
  - o a *global* attribution means that the behaviour is seen as affecting other parts of the relationship;
  - o a *specific* attribution means that it is considered only to apply to one particular aspect of the relationship.
- *Stability*: the extent to which behaviour is likely to change over time:
  - o a *stable* attribution means that the behaviour is assumed to be typical of that person and will affect how they will behave in future;
  - o a *specific* explanation means that it is a 'one-off' and unlikely to happen again.

Bradbury and Fincham (1990) suggest that there are significant differences in the way dissatisfied as opposed to satisfied couples see the causes of their partner's behaviour. Unhappy couples tend to view their partner's behaviour in a very negative light, even when the behaviour is one they would normally like (such as saying their partner is looking good). Happy couples, in contrast, view their partner's behaviour in a positive light, even when they don't particularly like the behaviour.

To be more specific, unhappy couples see any *undesirable* behaviour as:

- *Internal*: characteristic of the person.
- *Stable*: long-lasting.
- *Global*: as applying to other areas of the relationship.

In contrast, *desirable* behaviour is seen as:

- *External*: due to circumstances.
- *Unstable*: not the way the person usually behaves.
- *Specific*: Applying only to that particular circumstance.

Happy couples respond in a completely different way. They see *undesirable* behaviour as:

- *External*: situational.
- *Unstable*: temporary.
- *Specific*: unlikely to apply to other areas of the relationship.

And *desirable* behaviour as:

- *Internal*: characteristic of the person.
- *Stable*: likely to recur.
- *Global*: likely to apply to other areas of the relationship.

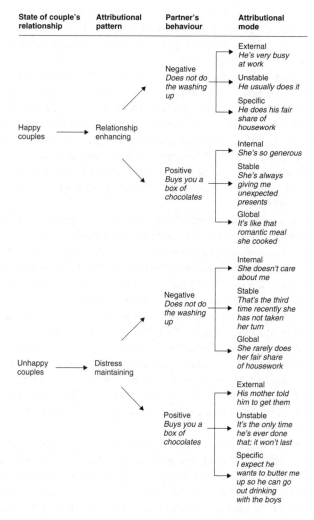

Figure 10.1 Attributional patterns used in happy and unhappy relationships.

The result of these attributions is that satisfied couples, by enhancing the impact of positive events whilst minimising the impact of negative ones, promote the well-being of the relationship. For example, Walter is especially quiet and preoccupied one evening; Emma takes the view that this is due to his not being selected for the local cricket team that week, not because he's losing interest in her. This attribution means his negative behaviour has no global implications for the marriage. Conversely unhappy couples maintain or increase dissatisfaction in their relationships by exaggerating the effect of negative events whilst diminishing the effect of positive one. Sue is late home from work one night and snappy. Mike believes this is because she cares more about work than spending time with him and that this, in turn, means that she no longer loves him. A string of such attributions is liable to move the marriage into a downward spiral.

Much research has established that there is an association between the attributions a spouse makes for events within the marriage and the couple's satisfaction (e.g. Bradbury & Fincham 1990; Bradbury et al. 2000; Fincham et al. 2000). Furthermore, it appears that the association is not a by-product of the spouse being depressed (Bauserman et al. 1995), angry (Senchak & Leonard 1993), having a negative outlook on life (Karney et al. 1994) or of violence within the marriage (Fincham et al. 1997). Moreover, this association is not culture specific (e.g. Sabourin et al. 1991).

The obvious question that arises is whether negative attributions cause marital unhappiness or whether the reverse is true. On the other hand, it is also possible that there is no direct causal link but, for example, a third factor is causing them both. Well, the answer is not straightforward: the exact role that attributions play in marital functioning is still a matter of research (see Bradbury et al. 2000, for a review). Nevertheless, there does appear to be a causal link that is bidirectional – they influence each other (Fincham et al. 2000; Fincham 2001). Making negative attributions causes marital unhappiness, and marital dissatisfaction causes negative attributions to be made. However, over time, attributions predict levels of marital satisfaction more than satisfaction predicts attributions (Karney & Bradbury 2000) so the type of attribution used probably has a greater effect on satisfaction than vice versa.

The obvious importance of attributions within marriage means that they feature prominently in programmes designed to address issues of marital satisfaction and prevent marital breakdown. Unfortunately little, if any, evaluation has been made of the importance of attitude change as a precursor to making progress in marital therapy (see Fincham et al. 1990).

The Vulnerability-Stress-Adaptation Model of marriage

The question remains as to why some couples enter a downward spiral of negative attributions whilst others continue to stay positive. It is inevitable that the rose-coloured spectacles will slip a little from all couples as they come across aspects of their partner's behaviour that they don't like, but in the early days most of them will make attributions that acknowledge their partner's shortcomings whilst maintaining an overall positive view of the marriage. Why does this change in some couples but not others?

Based on research on attributions described above, Karney and Bradbury (1995) offer an explanation in the form of the Vulnerability-Stress-Adaptation Model (the VSA model), which takes account of the broader context of the marriage – other family members, friends, the social milieu. This model suggests that when looking at the reasons for the attributions that couples make, we need to consider two general reasons:

1   The individuals themselves and their **enduring vulnerability** (e.g. childhood experiences, personality traits, cognitive styles). Adults who have had negative family experiences in childhood (whose parents have divorced or who have been raised in extremely unhappy and argumentative households) have great difficulty resolving problems within their relationships. These childhood experiences are believed to affect the extent to which people are capable of seeing two sides of an argument, how prepared they are to make compromises and how capable they are of jointly tackling marital problems in a constructive way (e.g. Story *et al*. 2004).

> **KEY TERMS**
>
> **Enduring vulnerability** Any persistent, long-term effects (such as childhood experiences, personality traits, cognitive styles) that may lead a person to be susceptible to stressful events.
>
> **Environmental stressors** Any external events (e.g. being made redundant, becoming seriously ill) that put a strain on a person and/or relationship.

2   The **environmental stressors** (e.g. stress at work, financial strains, health issues, concerns over extended family). The greater these are, the more likely they are to have a detrimental effect on the relationship.

Figure 10.2 shows how these two sets of factors interact.

When stress is low, couples tend to make positive attributions so that marriages survive and have reasonably high levels of satisfaction regardless of the characteristics of the individuals involved. It is during times of stress that the individual characteristics of the couple may make or break the relationship. Some people can manage to make

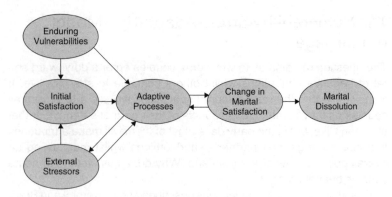

Figure 10.2 The Vulnerability-Stress-Adaptation Model of Marriage (Karney & Bradbury 1995).

positive attributions even during these times. Others, however, are unable to do this: they blame their partners for behaviour they previously excused and their negative attributions whittle away at the marriage, sometimes causing it to end in divorce.

To return to the question of why so many marriages show a significant drop in satisfaction levels, we can sum up as follows. After marriage, there are inevitable disappointments as the partner's shortcomings are recognised. Those individuals who show high levels of vulnerability cannot cope with these effectively. They begin to put negative interpretations on their partner's behaviour – and so the drop in satisfaction starts. Amongst couples who have low vulnerability levels, if the level of stress they encounter is very high then they find it difficult to respond well to challenging behaviour by their spouse and they too start making negative attributions, again initiating a downward spiral. In a sense, this may seem fairly obvious but it does have some serious implications for helping troubled marriages. Sometimes policies that try to address sources of stress in the marriage rather than focus on the relationship itself can be very effective. Bradbury and Karney (2010) point to research by Hardoy and Schøne (2008) showing that in Norway, after the government offered cash incentives to parents to stay at home with their children rather than use state-subsidised childcare, thereby reducing the stress of trying to juggle childcare with paid work, marital dissolution fell significantly in the short run.

Rusbult and Zembrodt's model of responses to relationship dissatisfaction

How do individuals respond when their relationship becomes unsatisfactory? Rusbult and Zembrodt (1983) proposed a model designed to classify the reactions of people when a relationship becomes miserable and to explain the circumstances under which each type of response is made. It is quite a general model, in that it applies to all types of relationships, including dissatisfaction in employer–employee relationships (Rusbult *et al.* 1988), but here we consider how it was originally applied to romantic relationships.

According to this model there are four main responses to relationship dissatisfaction, and these responses vary on two dimensions: *active* or *passive*, and *constructive* or *destructive*.

Figure 10.3 provides an illustration of this:

Voice

An active, constructive response. This includes discussing problems, suggesting compromise, seeking help, trying to change oneself or their partner or both.

Loyalty

A passive, constructive response. This is a supportive response in which the individual passively but optimistically waits for things to improve. Responses include deciding 'I'll give it some time', 'I'm going to try to forgive and forget'.

Neglect

A passive, destructive response. This involves refusing to deal with the problem, thus letting the situation deteriorate through lack of effort. Responses include ignoring the partner, spending less time with them,

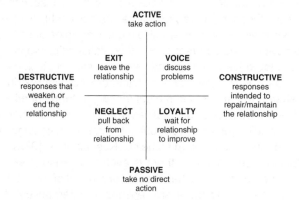

Figure 10.3 Responses to dissatisfaction in relationships (based on Rusbuldt and Zembrodt 1983).

criticising them (often behind their back), abusing them physically and /or emotionally, being unfaithful.

Exit

An active, destructive response. An exit response involves getting out of the relationship altogether. Exit responses include formal separation, moving out of the shared home, deciding to be 'just good friends', filing for divorce.

The dimension destructive–constructive refers to the effect *on the relationship* of a particular response: neglect and exit responses are liable to destroy the relationship, whereas voice and loyalty are aimed at maintaining it. Likewise, passive refers to the impact of the behaviour on the relationship itself rather than an individual's response. For example, a 'neglect' response such as criticising partner may be overtly active but it is passive and destructive in regard to the future of the relationship.

Based on social exchange principles (see Chapter 4) and specifically interdependence theory, there are three main factors that predict which of these responses is made:

1   The degree to which the individual is satisfied with the relationship prior to its decline.
2   The magnitude of the individual's investment of resources in the relationship.
3   The quality of the individual's best alternative to the current relationship.

The more satisfactory the relationship was before its decline, the more likely the individual is to use voice and loyalty. These constructive responses are those most likely to restore the relationship to its previous state. Constructive responses are also more likely to be used by individuals who have invested a great deal in the relationship, simply because they have a lot to lose by its breakdown. Investments include intrinsic ones such as self-disclosing and investing emotion and extrinsic ones such as shared resources and mutual friends. In terms of alternatives, one would expect that good alternatives would predict exit whereas poor alternatives would promote loyalty but not all research findings unequivocally support this even though some do (Rusbult *et al.* 1982).

Combining these together, there is evidence (Rusbult *et al.* 1982) that when the relationship has been very unsatisfactory, little has been invested in it and there are reasonable alternatives, the most likely response is exit. When relationship problems are considered to be relatively minor, and either there are few alternatives or there has been considerable investment (or both), the most popular response is loyalty. These researchers also found that women are more likely than men to use voice as are people who are well educated, while those with less education are more liable to respond by loyalty or neglect.

This model does provide a clear typology of responses to dissatis-faction in romantic relationships but it is fair to question whether these modes of behaving are the response to dissatisfaction with the rela-tionship or are in fact the causes of the problems (Duck 1988).

COMMENT AND DISCUSSION

Unrealistic relationship beliefs

To what extent do unrealistic beliefs about relationships contribute to people's lack of success in finding happiness in a relationship? Lar-son (1992) lists nine unrealistic beliefs that contribute to problems in relationships:

1   The 'one and only' belief: there is only one right person to marry.
2   The 'perfect partner' belief: the perfect partner must be found before you choose to marry.
3   The 'perfect self' belief: I must be perfect before I choose to marry.
4   The 'perfect relationship' belief: our relationship must be perfect before we marry.
5   The 'try harder' belief: it's possible to be happy in any relation-ship as long as you work hard at it.
6   The 'love is enough' belief: being in love is enough to make a marriage work.
7   The 'cohabitation' belief: living together will help prove our relationship before we marry.
8   The 'opposites complement' belief: opposites attract and work well together.
9   The 'choosing should be easy' belief: choosing a mate is a matter of chance and luck.

Research (some of which you will have come across in this book) demonstrates that none of these beliefs is true. Priest et al. (2009) demonstrated that experience in relationships tends to dispel these myths thus enabling people to go forward with a more realistic view of relationships.

What do you think?

The process of relationship dissolution

There are several models that look at the course taken when a relationship begins to deteriorate. A particularly influential one is that of Duck (1982), modified by Rollie and Duck (2006).

Duck's model of relationship dissolution

Duck (1982, 1988, 1992) argues that relationship breakdown is not a single event but a *process* that occurs in a systematic manner over a period of time.

In the original model, Duck suggests that there are four different phases involved in a relationship dissolution and that each of these phases is initiated when a certain threshold of dissatisfaction is reached. The Rollie and Duck (2006) modification of this model emphasised predominant processes rather than discrete phases and added an extra phase at the end, that of 'resurrection'.

The intrapsychic phase: focus on partner

This first, intrapsychic, phase begins when the threshold 'I can't stand it any more' is reached. One (or both) of the partners experiences dissatisfaction with how the relationship is going and spends a lot of time fretting about partner's faults and the disadvantages of the relationship. At this stage nothing is said to the partner, who may be oblivious to any problems.

The dyadic phase: focus on the relationship

When the threshold 'I'd be justified in withdrawing' is reached, the dyadic phase begins. If the relationship is not particularly formal, the end may be left implicit. Most of us are familiar with situations in which one party says something like 'I'll be in touch', 'I'll ring you', or the even vaguer 'See you around'. In relationships that involve marriage or cohabitation, the discontented party must face up to telling his or her partner. Once this declaration has been made, a lot of time is then spent discussing important issues: roles, equity, commitments to the relationship. These discussions begin to repair or break up the relationship.

The social phase: facing the public consequences

If the negotiations are unsuccessful so that the threshold of 'I mean it' is reached, the dissolution moves into the social phase. The dissatisfaction and plans for breakup now become public, and each partner confides in others in an attempt to enlist support for their version of events. There is still a possibility that things can be patched up and in some cases the parties may seek outside help (an 'intervention team') to try to put their side of the story to the other partner. If, however, the relationship does come to an end, it is essential that each party makes public a version of events that doesn't make them look as if they have behaved badly. Both in this social phase and in the next, gossip is an important means of spreading the word about the justification of actions taken.

The grave-dressing phase: tidying up the accounts

The final, grave-dressing phase begins once the threshold of 'It's now inevitable' is reached. As Duck (1992, p. 97) says,

> Once the relationship is dead we have to bury it 'good and proper' – with a tombstone saying how it was born, what it was like, and why it died. We have to create an account of the relationship's history and, as it were, put that somewhere so that other people can see it and, we hope, accept it.

One of the most important aspects of the grave-dressing (and the social) phase is that we leave the relationship without damaging our reputation. Duck points to the work of La Gaipa (1982) who says that once a relationship is over, we try to ensure that our 'social credit' is intact by taking little or no personal blame for the breakup. Either we blame conditions that existed before the start of the relationship, or external circumstances, or our partner, or any combination of these. Familiar types of comments made at this stage are: 'I really tried, but no matter what she says, I'm sure she had never really got over Gerry. I didn't stand a chance'; 'He was never at home, always in the pub while I was stuck in with the kids – that's no life'. The type of comment *not* made is: 'I'm basically a selfish pig. I never really gave a damn about him and once the novelty wore off, I fancied taking my chances in a new bed. I think monogamy is very overrated'. Such an ill-advised remark would, needless to say, seriously lower the amount of 'credit' that could be offered to a new relationship.

Resurrection phase

The emphasis in this phase is on how the partners prepare and launch themselves for future relationships. They now focus on what they have learnt from the mistakes of the previous relationship and how this will help them in future ones. They make further adaptation and adjustment to the demise of the relationship and the concomitant loss of a valued connection. In this way they gain self-knowledge and relationship-knowledge to help them in the future.

Duck (2007) argues that research has emphasised the processes involved in acquaintance and those involved in breakdown but has tended to overlook those involved in repair. This model, especially in its modified version, has some useful practical implications for the repair of relationships. It suggests that in some phases, certain strategies will be more effective than others in trying to put things right. For example, in the intrapsychic phase, repair should aim at re-establishing liking for the partner by keeping a record of their positive, pleasing aspects rather than dwelling on the negative. In addition, people should be encouraged to use more positive attributions towards their partner's behaviour and to make greater efforts to see things from their point of view. In the social phase, individuals outside the relationship (the intervention team) need to decide whether to advise the parties to try and repair the damage or if it would be better for the relationship to end with as much face saving as possible. In essence, in terms of repair, this model proposes that '... repairing of disrupted relationships will be most effective when it addresses the concerns that are most important to us at the process of dissolution of relationships which we have reached'. (Duck 2007, p. 101).

Duck (1982), among others, points out that there are certain problems with researching relationship dissolution. Although it is possible to study relationships at a time when problems become apparent, this is not usually done for fear that it may alter the course of events and perhaps precipitate a breakdown that may not otherwise have occurred. Most breakdowns are therefore studied in retrospect (after the event), which means that what actually happened is not always accurately recorded. For this reason it is possible that the very earliest stages of dissatisfaction tend not to be reported (Duck, 1982).

Positive Psychology: it's not all bad

The breakdown of a relationship is often a very distressing experience. It can initially result in negative reactions such as depression (Monroe *et al.* 1999), then loneliness, distress and loss of self (Lewandowski *et al.* 2006). However, the tacit assumption that such experiences are always negative is now being challenged, and there is increasing recognition that leaving a relationship can be a very liberating experience. Now that relationship dissolution is neither unusual nor greatly stigmatised, breaking down and patching up are becoming a major focus of relationship research.

The growing movement of **Positive Psychology** examines the positive elements of experiences that promote well-being and happiness. Although many relationship endings are shrouded in sadness and anger, not all of the experience is negative. Both positive emotion and the positive experience of self-growth and self-improvement do occur and may be quite common.

KEY TERM

Positive Psychology A movement within psychology that looks at positive elements of experience that promote well-being and happiness.

Most research shows that the occurrence of negative emotions far outweighs that of positive ones in the majority of breakups. However it may be possible to change this. In one study, in which participants were asked to write about a breakdown from personal experience and to think about positive elements to it, the number of positive emotions expressed outweighed the negative ones. Some individuals recognised that, having carried out such therapeutic exercises, they now felt more able to regulate their own emotions, had greater self-confidence and were better able to choose suitable partners (Lewandowski & Bizzoco 2007). Even when there is a great deal of emotional pain, people may develop skills that can be of use in making future relationships more satisfying (Fredrickson & Joiner 2002). The ability to cope with breakdown successfully is far greater if individuals can make a positive reinterpretation of the breakup experience rather than venting their negative emotions; this gives them greater resilience to withstand future disappointments of all kinds. In general, encouraging people to use positive emotions, including making plans for the future, can contribute hugely to an individual's future well-being.

Summary

- Divorce is a fairly common occurrence. In Britain, 33% of marriages end in divorce by the 15th anniversary; in the USA it is 43%. Most marriages show a decline in satisfaction over time, especially during the first 10 years.
- Conflict in relationships is a major source of dissatisfaction. Kurdek (1994) lists the six most common general issues causing conflict as power, social issues, personal flaws, distrust, intimacy, and personal distance.
- Attribution of behaviour is an important factor associated with dissatisfaction in marriage. In unhappy marriages, behaviour of the partner tends to be attributed negatively whereas in happy marriages it is attributed positively. At present it is not entirely clear whether negative attributions

cause dissatisfaction, whether the opposite is true or whether a third factor is responsible for both. Nevertheless, research indicates that both causal links are true – negative attributions cause marital discord and marital dissatisfaction results in negative attributions of behaviour. That said, negative attributions probably have a greater effect on satisfaction than vice versa.

- The Vulnerability-Stress-Adaptation (VSA) model of marriage states that both individual vulnerability to stress and outside stressors contribute to marital breakdown. The greater the outside stresses and the more vulnerable the individuals, the more likely the marriage is to be dissolved. Robust individuals cope with stress well, whilst marriages with little stress will survive even when the individuals are very susceptible to its effects.

- Rusbult and Zembrodt's model of relationship dissatisfaction suggests that there are four kinds of behaviour that people use to deal with relationship dissatisfaction: voice, exit, loyalty and neglect. These vary along two dimensions: destructive–constructive and active–passive.

- Duck's model of relationship dissolution proposes four phases in relationship breakdown. The intrapsychic phase is reached when one partner (or both) feels that they can't stand it anymore. The dyadic phase is precipitated by the feeling that a partner is justified in leaving. The social phase involves making this justification public and perhaps seeking outside help to put things right. In the grave-dressing phase the relationship is finally ended, with each partner making public a version of the breakdown that does not jeopardise their chances of developing a new relationship. The resurrection phase is a later addition to the model (Rollie & Duck 2006); it involves the partners preparing to launch themselves into future relationships.

FURTHER READING

Duck, S. (2007) *Human Relationships* (4th edn, Chapter 3). Thousand Oaks, CA: Sage.

Seligman, M. & Csikszentmihalyi, M. (2000) Positive psychology: An introduction. *American Psychologist, 55*(1), 5–14.

Snyder, C.R. (2002) *Handbook of Positive Psychology*. Oxford, UK: Oxford University Press.

References

Adams, R.E. & Laursen, B. (2007) The correlates of conflict: Disagreement is not necessarily detrimental. *Journal. of Family Psychology, 21*(3), 445–458

Adams, R.G. (1986) Friendship and aging. *Generations, 10*, 40–43.

Agnew, C.R., van Lange, P.A.M., Rusbult, C.E. & Langston, C.A. (1998) Cognitive interdependence: Commitment and the mental representation of close relationships. *Journal of Personality and Social Psychology, 74.* 939–954.

AhYun, K. (2002) Similarity and attraction. In M. Allen, R.W. Preiss, B.M. Gayle & N.A. Burrell (Eds.), *Interpersonal Communication Research* (pp. 145–167). Mahwah, NJ Lawrence Erlbaum Associates Inc.

Ainsworth, M.D.S., Blehar, M.C., Waters, E. & Wall, S. (1978) *Patterns of Attachment: A Psychological Study of the Strange Situation.* Hillsdale, NJ: Lawrence Erlbaum Associates Inc.

Altman, I., Vinsel, A. & Brown, B.A. (1981) Dialectic conceptions in social psychology: An application to social penetration and privacy regulation. In L. Berkowitz (Ed.), *Advances in Experimental Social Psychology* (Vol. 14). New York: Academic Press.

Altman, L. & Taylor, D.A. (1973) *Social Penetration.* New York: Holt, Rinehart, Winston.

Argyle, M. & Henderson, M. (1985) *The Anatomy of Relationships.* Harmondsworth, UK: Penguin.

Aronson, E. & Linder, D. (1965) Gain and loss of esteem as determinants of interpersonal attractiveness. *Journal of Experimental Social Psychology, 1*, 156–172.

Aronson, E. & Worchel, S. (1966) Similarity versus liking as determinants of interpersonal attractiveness. *Psychonomic Science, 5*, 157–158.

Aumer-Ryan, K., Hatfield, E. & Frey R. (2006) Equity in romantic relationships: An analysis across self-construal and culture. Unpublished manuscript. University of Texas, Austin, Texas.

Aumer-Ryan, K., Hatfield, E. & Frey R. (2007) Examining Equity theory across cultures. *Interpersona: An International Journal on Personal Relationships.* Available from www.interpersona.org

Back, M.D., Schmukle, S.C. & Egloff, B. (2008) Becoming friends by chance. *Psychological Science, 19*, 439–440.

Backman, C.W. & Secord, P.F. (1959). The effect of perceived liking on interpersonal attraction. *Human Relations, 12*, 379–384.

Baldwin, A., Baldwin, C. & Cole, R.E. (1990) Stress-resistant families and stress-resistant children. In J.E. Rolf, A.S. Masten, D. Cicchetti, K.N. Wech-terlein & S. Weintraub (Eds), *Risk and Protective Factors in the Development of Psychopathology* (pp. 257–280). New York: Cambridge University Press.

Baldwin, M.W. (1992) Relational schemas and the processing of social information. *Psychological Bulletin, 112*, 461–484

Batool, S. & Malik, N.I. (2010) Role of attitude similarity and proximity in interpersonal attraction among friends (C 310). *International Journal of Innovation, Management and Technology, 1* (2), 142–146.

Baumeister, R.F. & Leary, M.R. (1995) The need to belong: desire for interpersonal attachments as a fundamental human motivation. *Psychological Bulletin, 117*, 497–529.

Baumrind, D. (1973) The development of instrumental competence through socialization. In A.D. Pick (Ed.), *Minesota Symposium on Child Psychology* (pp. 3–46). Minneapolis: University of Minnesota Press.

Baumrind, D. (1991) Parenting styles and adolescent development. In J. Brooks-Gunn, R. Lerner & A.C. Peterson (Eds), *The Encyclopedia of Adolescence* (pp. 746–758). New York: Garland.

Bauserman., A.K. Arias, I. & Craighead, W.E. (1995) Marital attributions in spouses of depressed patients. *Journal of Psychopathology & Behavioural Assessment, 17*, 231–249.

Beach, S.R.H., Fincham, F.D. & Katz, J. (1998) Marital therapy in the treatment of depression: Toward a third generation of therapy and research. *Clinical Psychology Review, 18*, 635–661.

Beaujouan, E. & Bhrolcháin, M. (2011) Cohabitation and marriage in Britain since the 1970s. *Population Trends, 145*, 35–59.

Berg, J.H. (1987) Responsiveness and selfdisclosure. In V.J. Derlega & J.H. Berg (Eds), *Self-disclosure: Theory, Research and Therapy* (pp. 101–130). New York: Plenum.

Berger, D.G. & Wenger, M.G. (1973) The ideology of virginity. *Journal of Marriage and the Family, 35*, 666–676.

Berkman, L.F., Glass, T., Brissette, I. & Seeman, T.E. (2000) From social integration to health: Durkheim in the new millennium. *Social Science and Medicine, 51*, 843–857

Berkman, L.F. & Syme, L. (1979) Social networks, host resistance, and mortality: A nine-year follow-up study of Alameda County residents. *American Journal of Epidemiology, 117*, 1003–1009.

Berreman, G.D. (1962) Pahari Polyandry: A comparison. *American Anthropologist, 64*(1), 60–75.

Berscheid, E. (1983) Emotion. In H.H. Kelley, E. Berscheid, A. Christensen, J.H. Harvey, T.L. Huston, G. Levinger, E. McClintock, L.A. Peplau & D.R. Peterson (Eds.), *Close Relationships* (pp. 110–168). New York: Freeman.

Berscheid, E. & Walster, E. (1969) *Interpersonal Attraction*. Reading, MA: Addison-Wesley.

Berscheid, E. & Walster, E. (1978) *Interpersonal Attraction* (2nd edn). Reading, MA: Addison-Wesley.

Berscheid, E. & Reis, H. (1998) Attraction and close relationships. In T. Gilbert,

S.T. Fiske & G. Lindzey (Eds), *The Handbook of Social Psychology* (Vol. 2, 4th edn). New York: McGraw-Hill.

Berscheid, E., Synder, M., Omoto, A.M. (1989) The Relationship Closeness Inventory: Assessing the closeness of interpersonal relationships. *Journal of Personality & Social Psychology, 57,* 792–807.

Bibby, R.W. (2001) *Canada's Teens: Today, Yesterday, and Tomorrow.* Ottawa, Canada: Novalis.

Boase, J. Horrigan, J., Wellman, B. & Raine, L. (2006) *The Strength of Internet Ties.* Pew Internet & American Life Project, Washington, DC.

Boase, J. & Wellman, B. (2006) Personal relationships: On and off the internet. In D. Perlman & A.L. Vagelisti (Eds), *Handbook of Personal Relations.* Cambridge, UK: Cambridge University Press.

Bornstein, R.R., Kale, A.R. & Cornell, K.R. (1990) Boredom as limiting condition in the mere exposure effect. *Journal of Personality and Social Psychology, 58,* 791–800.

Bossard, J.H.S. (1932) Residential propinquity as a factor in marriage selection. *American Journal of Sociology, 38,* 219–224.

Bowlby, J. (1969) *Attachment and Loss: Vol 1. Attachment.* New York: Basic Books.

Bowlby, J. (1969/1982) *Attachment and Loss: Vol. 1. Attachment* (2nd ed). New York: Basic Books [new printing, 1999, with a foreword by Allan N. Schore; originally published in 1969].

Bowlby, J. (1973) *Attachment and Loss: Vol. 2. Separation, Anxiety, and Anger.* London: Penguin Books.

Bowlby, J. (1988) *A Secure Base: Clinical Applications of Attachment Theory.* London: Routledge.

Bradbury, T.N. & Fincham, F.D. (1990) Attributions in marriage: Review and critique. *Psychological Bulletin, 107,* 3–33.

Bradbury, T.N., Fincham, F.D. & Beach, S.R.H. (2000) Research on the nature and determinants of marital satisfaction. *Journal of Marriage and the Family, 62,* 964–980.

Bradbury, T.N. & Karney, B.R. (2010) *Intimate Relationships.* New York: W.W. Norton.

Bramlett, M.D. & Mosher, W.D. (2002) *Cohabitation, Marriage, Divorce, and Remarriage in the United States.* Vital and Health Statistics (Vol. 23, No. 22). Hyattsville, MD: National Center for Health Statistics.

Brehm, S.S. (1992) *Intimate Relationships.* New York: McGraw-Hill, Inc.

Brennan, K.A., Clark, C.L. & Shaver P.R. (1998) Self-report measurement of adult attachment: An integrative overview In J.A. Simpson & W.S. Rhodes (Eds) *Attachment Theory and Close Relationships* (pp. 46–76). New York: Guilford Press.

Brown, G.W., Andrews, B., Harris, T., Adler, Z. & Bridge, L. (1986) Social support, self-esteem and depression. *Psychological Medicine, 16,* 813–831.

Brown, G.W. & Harris, T. (1978) *Social Origins of Depression.* London: Tavistock.

Brummett, B.H., Barefoot, J.C., Siegler, I.C., Clapp-Channing, N.E., Lytle, B.L., Bosworth, H.B., Williams, R.B. & Mark, D.B. (2001) Characteristics of socially isolated patients with coronary artery disease who are at elevated risk for mortality. *Psychosomatic Medicine, 63,* 267–272.

Buck, R., & Ginsburg, B. (1997) Communicative genes and the evolution of empathy. In W. Ickes (Ed.) *Empathic Accuracy* (pp. 17–43). New York: Guilford.

Buote, V.M., Wood, E. & Pratt, M. (2009) Exploring similarities and differences between online and offline friendships: The role of attachment style. *Computers in Human Behavior, 25,* 560–567

Burk, W.J. & Laursen, B. (2005) Adolescent perceptions of friendship and their associations with individual adjustment. *International Journal of Behavioural Development, 29,* 156–164.

Burley, N. (1983). The meaning of assortative mating. *Ethology and Sociobiology, 4,* 191–203.

Buss, D.M. (1989) Sex differences in human mate preferences: Evolutionary hypotheses tested in 37 cultures. *Behavioral and Brain Sciences, 12,* 1–14.

Buunk, B.P. (1987) Conditions that promote break-ups as a consequence of extradyadic involveness. *Journal of Social and Clinical Psychology, 5,* 237–50.

Buunk, A.P. & Dijkstra, P. (2001) Evidence for a sex-based rival oriented mechanism: Jealousy as a function of a rival's physical attractiveness and dominance in a homosexual sample. *Personal Relationships, 8,* 391–406.

Buunk, B.P. & Van Yperen, N.W. (1989) Social comparison, equality, and relationship satisfaction: Gender differences over a ten-year period. *Social Justice Research, 3,* 157–180.

Buunk, B.P. & Van Yperen, N.W. (1991) Referential comparisons, relational comparisons, and exchange orientation: Their relation to marital satisfaction. *Personality and Social Psychology Bulletin, 17,* 709–717.

Byers, E.S. & Wang, A. (2004) Understanding sexuality in close relationships from the social exchange perspective. In J.H. Harvey, A. Wenzel & S. Sprecher (Eds), *Handbook of Sexuality in Close Relationships* (pp. 203–234). Mahwah, NJ: Lawrence Erlbaum Associates, Inc.

Byrne, D. (1971) *The Attraction Paradigm.* New York: Academic Press.

Byrne, D. Baskett, G.D. & Hodges, L. (1971) Behavioural indicators of interpersonal attraction. *Journal of Applied Social Psychology, 1,* 137–149.

Byrne, D., Clore, G.L. & Smeaton, G. (1986) The attraction hypothesis: Do similar attitudes affect anything? *Journal of Personality and Social Psychology, 51,* 1167–1170.

Cairncross, F. (1997) *The Death of Distance.* Boston, MA: Harvard Business School Press.

Campbell, L.D., Connidis, I.A. & Davies, L. (1999) Sibling ties in later life: A social network analysis. *Journal of Family Issues, 20* (1), 114–148.

Canary, D.J. & Stafford, L. (1992) Relational maintenance strategies and equity in marriage. *Communication Monographs, 59,* 243–267

Canary, D.J., Stafford, L., Hause, K.S. & Wallace, L.A. (1993) An inductive analysis of relational maintenance strategies: Comparisons among lovers, relatives, friends, and others. *Communication Research Reports, 10,* 5–14

Canary, D.J. & Stafford, L. (2001) Equity in the preservation of personal rela-
tionships. In J.H. Harvey & A. Wenzel (Eds), *Close romantic relationships:
Maintenance and enhancement* (pp. 133–151). Mahwah, NJ: Lawrence
Erlaum Associates, Inc.

Caporael, L.R. (2007) Evolutionary theory for social and cultural psychology. In
A.W. Kruglanski & E. Tory Higgins (Eds), *Social Psychology: Handbook of
Basic Principles* (2nd edn). Guilford Press: New York.

Carli, L.L., Ganley, R. & Pierce-Otay, A. (1991) Similarity and satisfaction in
roommate relationships. *Personality and Social Psychology Bulletin, 17,*
419–426.

Carson, R. (1969) *Interaction Concepts of Personality.* Chicago: Aldine.

Carson, J. & Parke, R.D. (1996) Reciprocal negative affect in parent-child
interactions and children's peer competency. *Child Development, 67,*
2217–2226.

Cate, R.M. & Lloyd, S.A. (1988) Courtship. In S. Duck (Ed.), *Handbook of Personal Relationships: Theory, Research and Intervention* (pp. 409–427).
New York: Wiley.

Cate, R.M. & Lloyd, S.A. (1992) *Courtship.* Newbury Park, CA: Sage.

Chao, R.K. (1994) Beyond parental control & authoritaritan parenting style:
Understanding Chinese parenting through the cultural notion of training.
Child Development, 65, 1111–1119.

Chapman, B. (1992) The Byrne–Clore formula revisited: The additional impact
of number of dissimilar attitudes on attraction. Unpublished Masters thesis,
University at Albany, State University of New York.

Chen, W. & Wellman, B. (2003) Fathoming the digital divide. In M. Romero &
E. Margolis (Eds), *Blackwell Handbook of Social Inequality.* Oxford, UK:
Blackwell.

Cherlin, A.J. (1992) *Marriage, Divorce, Remarriage.* Cambridge, MA: Harvard
University Press.

Chomsky, N. (1957) *Syntactic Structures.* The Hague: Mouton.

Clark, M.S. (1986) Evidence for the effectiveness of manipulations of communal and exchange relationships. *Personality and Social Psychology Bulletin,
12,* 414–425.

Clark, M.S. & Lemay, E.P., Jr. (2010) Close relationships. In S.T. Fiske, D.T.
Gilbert & G. Lindzey (Eds), *Handbook of Social Psychology* (5th edn, Vol. 2,
pp. 898–940). New York: Wiley.

Clark, M.S. & Mills, J. (1979) Interpersonal attraction in exchange and communal relationships. *Journal of Personality and Social Psychology, 37,* 12–24.

Cohen, S. & Hoberman, H.M. (1982) Positive events and social supports as
buffers on life change stress: Maximising the prediction of health outcome.
Unpublished manuscript, University of Oregon.

Collins, N.L. & Read, S.J. (1990) Adult attachment, working models, and the
relationship quality in dating couples. *Journal of Personality & Social Psychology, 58,* 644–663.

Condon, W.S. & Sandor, L. (1974) Neonate movement is synchronised with
adult speech: Interactional participation and language acquisition. *Science,
183,* 99–101.

Cramer, D. (1987) Lovestyles revisited, *Social Behaviour and Personality, 15,* 215–218.

Cramer, D. (1998) *Close Relationships: The Study of Love and Friendship.* New York: Arnold

Cunningham, M.R., Roberts, A.R., Barbee, A.P., Druen, P.B. & Wu, C.-H. (1995) 'Their ideas of beauty are, on the whole, the same as ours': Consistency and variability in the crosscultural perception of female physical attractiveness. *Journal of Personality and Social Psychology, 68,* 261–279.

Curtis, R.C. & Miller, K. (1986) Believing another likes or dislikes you: Behaviors making the beliefs come true. *Journal of Personality and Social Psychology, 51,* 284–290.

Dainton, M. (2011) Linking theoretical explanations for the use of marital maintenance equity, uncertainty, attachment, and reciprocity. *Acta de Investigacion Psicologica, 1*(2), 352–374.

Dainton, M. & Aylor, B.A. (2001) A relational uncertainty analysis of jealousy, trust, and the maintenance of long-distance versus geographically-close relationships. *Communication Quarterly, 49,* 172–188.

Dainton, M. & Stafford, L. (1993) Routine maintenance behaviors: A comparison of relationship type, partner similarity, and sex differences. *Journal of Social & Personal Relationships, 10,* 255–272.

Daly, M. & Wilson, M. (1983) *Sex, Evolution, and Behaviour* (2nd edn). Belmont, CA: Wadworth.

Davis, D. (1982) Determinants of responsiveness in dyadic interaction. In W.I. Icles & E.S. Knowles (Eds.), *Personality, Roles and Social Behaviours* (pp. 85–139). New York: Springer-Verlag

Davis, S. (1990) Men as success objects and women as sex objects: A study of personal advertisements. *Sex Roles, 23,* 43–50.

DeMaris, A. & Longmore, M.A. (1996) Ideology, power, and equity: Testing competing explanations for the perception of fairness in household labor. *Social Forces, 74,* 1043–1071.

Derber, C. (2000) *The Pursuit of Attention: Power and Ego in Everyday Life.* Oxford, UK: Oxford University Press.

Derlega, V.J., Metts, S., Petronio, S. & Margulis, S.T. (1993) *Self-disclosure.* Newbury Park, CA: Sage.

Dermer, M. & Thiel, D.L. (1975) When beauty may fail. *Journal of Personality and Social Psychology, 31,* 1168–1176.

Deutsch, M. & Collins, M.E. (1951) *Interracial Housing: A Psychological Evaluation of a Social Experiment.* Minneapolis: University of Minnesota Press.

De Waal, F. (1983) *Chimpanzee Politics: Power and Sex Among Apes.* New York: Harper & Row.

Dijkstra, P. & Buunk, A.P. (2002) Sex differences in the jealousy evoking effect of 56 rival characteristics. *European Journal of Social Psychology, 32*(6), 829–852.

Dion, K.K. & Berscheid, E. (1974) Physical attractiveness and peer perception among children. *Sociometry, 37,* 1–12.

Dion, K.K. & Dion, K.L. (1993) Individualistic and collectivist perspectives on gender and the cultural context of love and intimacy. *Journal of Social Issues*, *49*(3), 53–69.

Doi, L.T. (1963) Some thoughts on helplessness and the desire to be loved. *Psychiatry*, *26*, 266–272.

Doi, L.T. (1973) *The Anatomy of Dependence* (J. Bester, Trans.). Tokyo: Kodansha International.

Duck, S.W. (1982) *Personal Relationships 4: Dissolving Personal Relationships*. London and New York: Academic Press.

Duck, S. (1988) *Relating to Others*. Milton Keynes, UK: Open University Press.

Duck, S. (1991) *Friends, for Life: The Psychology of Personal Relationships* (2nd edn). London: Harvester Wheatsheaf

Duck, S. (1992) *Human Relationships* (2nd edn). London: Sage.

Duck, S. (1994) *Meaningful Relationships*. London: Sage.

Duck, S. (1995) Repelling the study of attraction. *The Psychologist*, *8*(2), 60–63.

Duck, S. (2007) *Human Relationships* (4th edn). London: Sage

Duck, S.W. & Wright, P. (1993) Reexamining gender differences in same-gender friendships: A close look at two kinds of data. *Sex Roles*, *28*, 709–727.

Dunn, J. & Munn, P. (1986) Sibling quarrels and maternal intervention: Individual differences in understanding and aggression. *Journal of Child Development Psychology & Psychiatry & Allied Disciplines*, *27*, 583–595.

Dunn, J. (2004) *Children's Friendships: The Beginning of Intimacy*. Oxford, UK: Blackwell.

Durkin, K. (1995) *Developmental Social Psychology*. Oxford, UK: Blackwell.

Dwyer, D. (2000) *Interpersonal relationships*. London: Routledge

Dwyer, D. & Roberts, C. (2009) *Psychology for GCSE Level* (2nd edn). Hove, UK: Psychology Press.

Eagly, H., Ashmore, D., Makhijani, M. & Longo, C. (1991) What is beautiful is good: A meta-analytic review of research on the physical attractiveness stereotype. *Psychology Bulletin*, *110*, 107–128.

Eagly, A.H. & Wood, W. (1999) The origins of sex differences in human behavior: Evolved dispositions versus social roles. *American Psychologist*, *54*, 408–423.

Eastwick, P.W. & Finkel, E.J. (2008) Sex differences in mate preferences revisited: Do people know what they initially desire in a romantic partner? *Journal of Personality and Social Psychology*, *95*, 628–647.

Ebbesen, E.B., Kjos, G.L. & Konecni, V.J. (1976) Spatial ecology: Its effects on the choice of friends and enemies. *Journal of Experimental Social Psychology*, *12*, 505–518.

Ellis, S., Rogoff, B. & Cromer, C.C. (1981) Age segregation in children's social interaction. *Developmental Psychology, 17*, 399–407.

Ertel K.A, Glymour M. & Berkman L.F. (2009) Social networks and health: A life course perspective integrating observational and experimental evidence. *Journal of Social and Personal Relationships*, *26*, 73–92.

Everson-Rose S.A, Lewis T.T. (2005) Psychosocial factors and cardiovascular diseases. *Annual Review of Public Health*, *26*, 469–500.

Fantz, R.L. (1961) The origin of form perception. *Scientific American*, *204*, 66–72.

Farah, M.J. (2000) *The Cognitive Neuroscience of Vision*. Malden, MA: Blackwell.

Farr, W. (1975) Marriage and mortality. In N. Humphreys (Ed.), *Vital Statistics: A Memorial Volume of Selections from the Reports and Writings of William Farr*. Metuchen, NJ: Scarecrow Press. (Original work published 1885.)

Farrer, J., Tsuchiya, H. & Bagrowitcz, B. (2008) Emotional expression in *tsukiau* dating relationships in Japan *Journal of Social and Personal Relationships*, *25*, 169–188.

Feingold, A. (1988) Matching for attractiveness in romantic partners and same-sex friends: A meta-analysis and theoretical critique. *Psychological Bulletin*, *104*(2), 226–235.

Felmlee, D. (1998) Fatal attraction. In B.H. Spitzberg & W.R. Cupach (Eds), *The Dark Side of Close Relationships* (pp. 3–31). Mahwah, NJ: Lawrence Erlbaum Associates Inc.

Felmlee, D. & Muraco, A. (2009) Same and cross-gender friendship norms among older adults. *Research on Aging*, *31*, 318–344.

Felmlee, D., Sprecher, S. & Bassin, E. (1990) The dissolution of intimate relationships: A hazard model. *Social Psychology Quarterly*, *53*, 13–30.

Festinger, L. (1954) A theory of social comparison processes. *Human Relations*, *7*, 117–40.

Festinger, L., Schachter, S. & Back, K.W. (1950) *Social Pressures in Informal Groups: A Study of Human Factors in Housing*. New York: Harper.

Ficara, L.C. & Mongeau, P.A. (2000 November) Relational uncertainty in long-distance college student dating relationships. Paper presented at the National Communication Association annual conference, Seattle, WA.

Finch, J. & Mason, J. (1993) *Negotiating Family Responsibilities*. London: Routledge

Fincham, F.D. (1997) Understanding marriage: From fish scales to milliseconds. *The Psychologist* 10 (12) (December).

Fincham, F.D. (2001) Attributions in close relationships: From balkanization to integration. In G.J. Fletcher & M. Clark (Eds), *Blackwell Handbook of Social Psychology* (pp. 3–31). Oxford, UK: Blackwell.

Fincham, F.D. & Beach, S.R. (1999) Conflict in marriage: Implications for working with couples. *Annual Review of Psychology*, *50*, 47–77.

Fincham, F.D., Bradbury, T.N., Arias, I., Byrne, C.A. & Karney, B.R. (1997) Marital violence, marital distress and attributions. *Journal of Family Psychology*, *11*, 367–372.

Fincham, F.D., Bradbury, T.N. & Beach, S.R. (1990) To arrive where we began: A reappraisal of cognition in marriage and marital therapy. *Journal of Family Psychology*, *4*, 167–184.

Fincham, F.D., Harold, G.T. & Gano-Phillips, S. (2000) The Longitudinal association between attributions and marital satisfaction: Direction of effects and role of efficacy expectations. *Journal of Family Psychology*, *14*, 267–285

Fisher, H. (1992) *The Anatomy of Love: A Natural History of Mating, Marriage, and Why We Stray*. New York Fawcett Columbine.

Fitzpatrick, M.A. & Badzinski, D.M. (1994) All in the family: Interpersonal communication in kin relationships. In M.L. Knapp & G.R. Miller (Eds), *Handbook of interpersonal communication* (2nd edn, pp. 726–771). Thousand Oaks, CA: Sage.

Foa, U.G. & Foa, E.B. (1974) *Societal Structures of the Mind*. Springfield, IL: Thomas.

Fortunato, L. & Archetti, M. (2010) Evolution of monogamous marriage by maximization of inclusive fitness. *Journal of Evolutionary Biology*, *23*, 149–156.

Fox, S. (1980) Situational determinants in affiliation. *European Journal of Social Psychology*, *10*, 303–307.

Fraley, R.C. & Spieker, S.J. (2003) Are infant attachment patterns continuously or categorically distributed? A taxometric analysis of strange situation behavior. *Developmental Psychology*, *39*, 387–404.

Fredrickson, B. & Joiner, T. (2002) Positive emotions trigger upward spirals toward emotional well-being. *Psychological Science*, *13*(2), 172–175.

Frisco, M.L. & Williams, K. (2003) Perceived housework equity, marital happiness, and divorce in dual-earner households. *Journal of Family Issues*, *24*, 51–73.

Fruzzetti, A.E. (1996) Causes and consequences: Individual distress in the context of couple interactions. *Journal of Consulting and Clinical Psychology*, *64*, 1192–1201.

Furnham, A., Tan, T. & McManus, C. (1997) Waist-to-hip ratio and preferences for body shape: A replication and extension. *Personality and Individual Differences*, *22*, 549.

Gager, C.T. & Sanchez, L. (2003) Two as one? Couples' perceptions of time spent together, marital quality, and the risk of divorce. *Journal of Family Issues*, *24*, 21–50.

Gazzaniga, M.S., Ivry, R.B. & Mangun, G.R. (1998) *Cognitive Neuroscience: The Biology of the Mind*. New York: Norton.

Geiselman, R., Haight, N. & Kimata, L. (1984) Context effects on the perceived physical attractiveness of faces. *Journal of Experimental Social Psychology*, *20*(5), 409–424.

Ghimire, D., Axinn, W., Yabiku, S. & Thornton, A. (2006) Social change, premarital nonfamily experience, and spouse choice in an arranged marriage society. *American Journal of Sociology*, *111*(4), 1181–1218.

Glenn, N.D. (1989) Duration of marriage, family consumption, and marital happiness. *National Journal of Sociobiology*, *3*, 3–24.

Glenn, N.D. (1998) The course of marital success and failure in five American 10-year marriage cohorts. *Journal of Marriage and the Family*, *60*, 569–576.

Goetting, A. (1986) The developmental tasks of siblingship over the life cycle. *Journal of Marriage and the Family*, *48*, 703–714.

Goleman, D. (1990) Support groups may do more in cancer than relieve the mind, *New York Times*, 18 October.

Gouldner, A.W. (1960) The norm of reciprocity: A preliminary statement. *American Sociological Review*, *25*, 161–178.

Gove, W.R. (1972) The relationship between sex roles, marital status and mental illness. *Social Forces, 51*, 34–44.

Grimes, C.L., Klein, T.R. & Puttallaz, M. (2004) Parents' relationships with their parents and peers: Influences on children's development. In J. Kupersmidt & K. Dodge (Eds), *Children's Peer Relations* (pp. 141–158). Washington, DC :American Psychological Association.

Grote, N.K. & Clark, M.S. (2004) Distributive justice norms and family work: What is perceived as ideal, what is applied, and what predicts perceived fairness. *Social Justice Research, 11*, 243–269.

Guerrero, L.K. & Bachman, G.F. (2006) Associations among relational maintenance behaviors, attachment-style categories, and attachment dimensions. *Communication Studies, 57*, 341–361.

Guerrero, L.K., Eloy, S.V. & Wabnik, A.I. (1993) Linking maintenance strategies to relationship development and disengagement: A reconceptualization. *Journal of Social & Personal Relationships, 10*, 273–283.

Gupta, U. & Singh, P. (1982) An exploratory study of love and liking and types of marriage. *Indian Journal of Applied Psychology, 19*, 92–97.

Gustavsson, L., Johnsson, J.I. & Uller, T. (2008) Mixed support for sexual selection theories of mate preferences in the Swedish population. *Evolutionary Psychology, 6*(4), 575–585

Haas, S.M. & Stafford, L. (1998) An initial examination of maintenance behaviors in gay and lesbian relationships. *Journal of Social and Personal Relationships, 15*, 846–855.

Hagen, R. & Kahn, A. (1975) Discrimination against competent women. Paper presented at meeting of Midwestern Psychological Association, Chicago, IL.

Hardoy, I. & Schøne, P. (2008) Subsidizing 'stayers'? Effects of a Norwegian child care reform on marital stability. *Journal of Marriage and Family, 70*, 571–584.

Harkless, L.E. & Fowers, B.J. (2005) Similarities and differences in relational boundaries among heterosexuals, gay men, and lesbians. *Psychology of Women Quarterly, 29*(2), 167–176.

Harmon-Jones, E. & Allen, J.B. (2001) The role of affect in the mere exposure effect: Evidence from psychophysiological and individual differences approaches. *Personality & Social Psychology Bulletin, 27*, 889–898.

Harris, L.T., McClure, S., van den Bos, W., Cohen, J. & Fiske, S.T. (2007) Regions of MPFC differentially turned to social and non-social affective evaluation. *Cognitive, Affective, & Behavioral Neuroscience, 7*, 309–316.

Harrist, A.W., Pettit, G.S., Dodge, K.A. & Bates, J.E. (1994) Dyadic synchrony in mother-child interaction: Relation with children's subsequent kindergarten development. *Family Relations, 43*, 417–424

Hart, C.H., Yang, C., Nelson, D.A., Jin, S., Bazarshaya, N., Nelson, L.J., Wu, X. & Wu, P. (1998) Peer contact patterns, parenting practices and preschoolers' competence in China, Russia, and the United States. In P. Slee & K. Rigby (Eds), *Peer Relations Among Children: Current Issues and Future Directions* (pp. 3–30). London, UK: Routledge.

Hartup, W.W. (1992) Friendships and their developmental significance. In M.

McGurk (Ed.), *Childhood Social Development: Contemporary Perspectives*. Hove, UK: Erlbaum.

Hassin, R. & Trope, Y. (2000) Facing faces: Studies on the cognitive aspects of physiognomy. *Journal of Personal and Social Psychology*, *78*(5), 837–852.

Hatfield, E., Greenberger, E., Traupmann, J. & Lambert, P. (1982) Equity and sexual satisfaction in recently married couples. *Journal of Sex Research*, *18*, 18–32.

Hatfield, E. & Rapson, R.L. (2002) Passionate love and sexual desire: Cross-cultural and historical perspectives. In A. Vangelisti, H.T. Reis, & M.A. Fitzpatrick (Eds), *Stability and Change in Relationships* (pp. 306–324). Cambridge, UK: Cambridge University Press.

Hatfield, E. & Rapson, R.L. (1993) *Love, Sex, and Intimacy: Their Psychology, Biology, and History*. New York: HarperCollins.

Hatfield, E., Rapson, R.L., Aumer-Ryan, K. (2008) Social justice in love relationships. Recent developments. *Social Justice Research*, *21*, 413–431.

Hatfield, E. & Sprecher, S. (1986) Measuring passionate love in intimate relations. *Journal of Adolescence*, *9*, 383–410.

Hatfield, E., Traupmann, J., Sprecher, S., Utne, M.K. & Hay, J. (1985) Equity and intimate relations: Recent research. In W. Ickles (Ed.), *Compatible and Incompatible Relationships*. New York: Springer-Verlag.

Hatfield, E., Utne, M.K. & Traupmann, J. (1979) Equity theory and intimate relationships. In R.L. Burgess & T.L. Huston (Eds), *Social Exchange in Developing Relationships*. New York: Academic Press.

Hatfield, E. & Walster, G.W. (1978) *A New Look at Love*, Reading, MA: Addison-Wesley.

Hayduk, L.A. (1983) Personal space: where we now stand. *Psychological Bulletin*, *94*, 293–335.

Hays, R.B., (1988) Friendship. In S. Duck (Ed.), *Handbook of Personal Relationships: Theory, Research, and Interventions* (pp. 391–408). Chicester, UK, Wiley.

Hazan, C., Hutt, M.J. & Markus, H. (1991) Continuity and change in inner working models of attachment. Unpublished manuscript, Department of Human Development, Cornell University, Ithaca, NY.

Hazan, C. & Shaver, P. (1987) Romantic love conceptualized as an attachment process. *Journal of Personality and Social Psychology*, *52*, 511–524.

Hazan, C. & Shaver, P. (1990) Love and work: An attachment-theoretical perspective. *Journal of Personality and Social Psychology*, *59*, 270–280.

Heine, S.J. & Lehman, D.R. (1995) Cultural variation in unrealistic optimism: Does the West feel more invulnerable than the East? *Journal of Personality and Social Psychology*, *68*, 595–607.

Hendrick, C. & Hendrick, S. (1986) A theory and method of love. *Journal of Personality & Social Psychology*, *50*(2), 392–402.

Hendrick, C. & Hendrick, S. (1989) Research on love: Does it measure up? *Journal of Personality and Social Psychology*, *56*, 784–794.

Hendrick, C. & Hendrick, S. & Adler, N. (1988) Romantic relationships: Love, satisfaction and staying together. *Journal of Personality & Social Psychology*, *54*(6), 980–988.

Hendrick, C., Hendrick, S. & Dicke, A. (1998) The Love Attitudes Scale: Short form. *Journal of Personal and Social Relationships, 15*, 147–159.

Hendrick, C., Hendrick, S.S., Foote, F.H. & Slapion-Foote, M.J. (1984) Do men and women love differently? *Journal of Social and Personal Relationships, 1*, 177–195.

Hill, C.A. (1987) Affiliation motivation: People who need people... but in different ways. *Journal of Personality and Social Psychology, 52*, 1008–1018.

Hill, C.T. & Peplau, L.A. (1998) Premarital predictors of relationship outcomes: A 15-year followup of the Boston Couples Study. In T.N. Bradbury (Ed.), *The Developmental Course of Marital Dysfunction* (pp. 237–278). New York: Cambridge University Press.

Hofstede, G. (1984) *Culture's Consequences*. Beverley Hills, CA: Sage.

Hogg, M.A. & Tindale, R.S. (Eds) (2001) *Blackwell Handbook of Social Psychology: Group Processes*. Oxford, UK: Blackwell.

Homans, G.C. (1961) *Social Behaviour*. New York: Harcourt, Brace & World.

House, J.S., Landis, K.R. & Umberson, D. (1988) Social relationships and health. *Science, 241*, 540–545.

Hsu, F. (1971) Filial piety in Japan and China. *Journal of Comparative Family Studies, 2*, 67–74.

Hsu, F.L.K. (1985) The self in cross-cultural perspective. In A.J. Marsella, G. DeVos, & F.L.K. Hsu (Eds), *Culture and Self: Asian and Western Perspectives* (pp. 24–55). London: Tavistock.

Hu, Y. & Goldman, N. (1990) Mortality differentials by marital status: An international comparison. *Demography, 27*, 233–250.

Hughes M.E. & Waite L.J. (2009) Marital biography and health at mid-life. *Journal of Health and Social Behavior, 50*, 344–358.

Huston, T.L., Caughlin, J.P., Houts, R.M., Smith, S.E. & George, L.J. (2001) The connubial crucible: Newlywed years as predictors of marital delight, distress, and divorce. *Journal of Personality and Social Psychology, 80*, 237–252.

Jackson, L.A., Hunter, J.E. & Hodge, C.N. (1995) Physical attractiveness and intellectual competence: A meta-analytic review. *Social Psychology Quarterly, 58*(2), 108–122.

Jankowiak, W.R. & Fischer, E.F. (1992) A cross-cultural perspective on romantic love. *Ethology, 31*, 149–155.

Johnson, D.J. & Rusbult, C.E. (1989) Resisting temptation: devaluation of alternative partners as a means of maintaining commitment in close relationships. *Journal of Personality and Social Psychology, 57*, 967–980.

Jones, E.E. (1964) *Ingratiation: A Social Psychological Analysis*. New York: Appleton-Century-Crofts.

Jones, J.T., Pelham, B.W., Carvallo, M. & Mirenberg, M.C. (2004) How do I love thee? Let me count the Js: Implicit egotism and interpersonal attraction. *Journal of Personality and Social Psychology, 87*, 665–683.

Kaiser Family Foundation. (2001) *Inside-Out: A Report on the Experiences of Lesbians, Gays and Bisexuals in America and the Public's View on Issues and Policies Related to Sexual Orientation*. Menlo Park, CA: Kaiser Family Foundation.

Kaplin, R.M. & Kronick, R.G. (2006) Marital status and longevity in the United States population. *Journal of Epidemiology and Community Health*, *60*, 760–765. doi:10.1136/jech.2005.037606

Karney, B.R. & Bradbury, T.N. (1995) The longitudinal course of marital quality and stability: A review of theory, methods, and research. *Psychological Bulletin*, *118*, 3–34.

Karney, B.R. & Bradbury, T.N. (2000) Attributions in marriage: State or trait? A growth curve analysis. *Journal of Personality and Social Psychology*, *78*, 295–309.

Karney, B.R., Bradbury, T.N., Fincham, F.D. & Sullivan, K.T. (1994) The role of negative affectivity in the association between attributions and marital satisfaction. *Journal of Personality and Social Psychology*, *66*, 413–424.

Kassel, J.D, Stroud, L.R. & Paronis, C.A. (2003) Smoking, stress, and negative affect: Correlation, causation, and context across stages of smoking. *Psychological Bulletin*, *129*, 270–304.

Keeley, M. & Hart, A.J. (1994) Nonverbal behavior in dyadic interactions. In S. Duck (Ed.), *Dynamics of Relationships* (pp. 135–179). Thousand Oaks, C.A: Sage.

Kelley, H.H., Berscheid, E., Christensen, A., Harvey, J.H., Huston, T.L., Levinger, G., McClintock, E., Peplau, L.A. & Peterson, D.R. (Eds) (1983) *Close Relationships*. New York: W.H. Freeman.

Kendel, D. (1978) Similarity in real-life adolescent friendship pairs. *Journal of Personality and Social Psychology*, *36*, 306–312.

Kenrick, D.T. & Trost, M.R. (1989) A reproductive exchange model of heterosexual relationships. In C. Hendrick (Ed.), *Close Relationships. Review of Personality and Social Psychology*. Newbury Park, CA: Sage.

Kephart, W.M. (1967) Some correlates of romantic love. *Journal of Marriage and the Family*, *29*, 470–474.

Kerckhoff, A.C. & Davis, K.E. (1962) Value consensus and need complementarity in mate selection, *American Sociological Review*, *27*, 295–303.

Kiecolt-Glaser, J.K., McGuire, L., Robles, T.R. & Glaser, R. (2002) Emotions, morbidity, and mortality: New perspectives from psychoneuroimmunology. *Annual Review of Psychology*, *53*, 83–107.

Kiecolt-Glaser, J.K., Gouin, J.P. & Hantsoo, L.V. (2010) Close relationships, inflammation, and health. *Neuroscience and Biobehavioral Reviews*, *35*, 33–38.

Kirkpatrick, L.A. & Hazan, C. (1994) Attachment styles and close relationships: A four-year prospective study. *Personal Relationships*, *1*, 123–142.

Kitzinger, C. & Wilkinson, S. (2004) The rebranding of marriage. *Feminism & Psychology*, *14*(1), 127–150.

Klinger, E. (1977) *Meaning and Void: Inner Experience and the Incentives in People's Lives*. Minneapolis: University of Minnesota Press.

Krueger, R.F., Moffitt, T.E., Caspi, A., Bleske, A. & Silva, P.A. (1998) Assortative mating for antisocial behavior: Developmental and methodological implications. *Behavior Genetics*, *28*, 173–186.

Kulik, J.A. & Mahler, H.I.M. (1989) Effects of preoperative roommate assignment on preoperative anxiety and recovery from coronary-bypass surgery, *Health Psychology*, *6*, 525–544.

Kupersmidt, J.B, Rosier, M.E. & Patterson, C.P. (1995) Similarity as a basis for children's friendships. The roles of sociomatric status, aggressive and withdrawal behavior, academic achievement, and demographic characteristics. *Journal of Social and Personal Relations*, *12*, 439–452.

Kurdek, L.A. (1991) Correlates of relationship satisfaction in cohabiting gay and lesbian couples. *Journal of Personality and Social Psychology*, *61*, 910–922.

Kurdek, L.A. (1993) The allocation of household labor in gay, lesbian, and heterosexual married couples. *Journal of Social Issues*, *49*(3), 127–139.

Kurdek, L.A. (1994) Areas of conflict for gay, lesbian and heterosexual couples: What couples agree about influences relationship satisfaction. *Journal of Marriage and the Family*, *56*, 297–313.

Kurdek, L.A. (1998) Relationship outcomes and their predictors: Longitudinal evidence from heterosexual married, gay cohabiting, and lesbian cohabiting couples. *Journal of Marriage and Family*, *60*, 553–568

Kurdek, L.A. (2004) Are gay and lesbian cohabiting couples *really* different from heterosexual married couples? *Journal of Marriage and Family*, *66*, 880–900

Kurdek, L.A. (2005) What do we know about gay and lesbian couples? *Current Directions in Psychological Science*, *14*, 251–254

Kurdek, L.A. (2006) Differences between partners from heterosexual, gay, and lesbian cohabiting couples. *Journal of Marriage and Family*, *68*, 509–528

Kurdek, L.A. & Schmitt, J.P. (1987) Partner homogamy in married, heterosexual cohabitating, gay, and lesbian couples. *Journal of Sex Research*, *23*(2), 212–232

La Gaipa, J.J. (1982) Rituals of disengagement. In S.W. Duck (Ed.), *Personal Relationships: Vol. 4. Dissolving Personal Relationships*. London: Academic Press.

Langlois, J.H., Kalakanis, L., Rubenstein, A.J., Larson, A., Hallam, M. & Smoot, M. (2000) Maxims or myths of beauty? A meta-analytic and theoretical review. *Psychological Bulletin*, *126*, 390–423.

Larson, J.H. (1992) 'You're my one and only': Premarital counseling for unrealistic beliefs about mate selection. *American Journal of Family Therapy*, *20*, 242–253.

Latané, B., Liu, J., Nowak, A., Bonavento, M. & Zheng, L. (1995) Distance matters: Physical distance and social impact. *Personality and Social Psychology Bulletin*, *21*, 795–805.

Laurenceau, J.-P., Feldman Barrett, L. & Pietromonaco, P.R. (1998) Intimacy as an interpersonal process: The importance of self-disclosure, and perceived partner responsiveness in interpersonal exchanges. *Journal of Personality and Social Psychology*, *74*, 1238–1251.

Laurenceau, J.-P., Feldman Barrett, L. & Rovine, M.J. (2005) The Interpersonal Process Model of intimacy in marriage: A daily-diary and multilevel modeling approach. *Journal of Family Psychology*, *19*(2), 314–323.

Leary, M.R., Rogers, P.A., Canfield, R.W. & Coe, C. (1986) Boredom in interpersonal encounters: Antecedents and social implications. *Journal of Personality and Social Psychology*, *51*(5), 968–975.

Lee, J.A. (1973) *Colours of Love*. Toronto: New Press.

Leigh, G.K., Homan, T.B. & Burr, W.R. (1987) Some confusions and exclusions of the SVR theory of dyadic pairing: A response to Murstein. *Journal of Marriage and the Family*, *49*, 933–937.

Lenhart, A. & Madden, M. (2007) *Social Networking Websites and Teens: An Overview*. Pew Internet & American Life Project. Washington, DC.

Leonard, R.L. jr. (1975) Self concept and attraction for similar and dissimilar others. *Journal of Personality and Social Psychology*, *31*, 926–929.

Lever, J. (1978) Sex differences in the complexity of children's play and games. *American Sociological Review*, *43*, 471–483.

Lever, J. (1994) The 1994 *Advocate* survey of sexuality and relationships: The men. *The Advocate: The National Gay & Lesbian Newsmagazine*, August 23, pp. 17–24.

Lever, J. (1995) The 1995 *Advocate* survey of sexuality and relationships: The women. *The Advocate: The National Gay & Lesbian Newsmagazine*, August 22, pp. 22–30.

Levine, R., Sato, S., Hashimoto, T. & Verma, J. (1995) Love and marriage in eleven cultures. *Journal of Cross-Cultural Psychology*, *26*, 554–571.

Levinger, G. (1976) A social psychological perspective on marital dissolution. *Journal of Social Issues*, *32*(1), 21–47.

Levinger, G., Senn, D.J. & Jorgensen, B.W. (1970) Progress toward permanence in courtship: A test of Kerchoff–Davis hypothesis. *Sociometry*, *33*, 427–443.

Levitt, M.J. (1991) Attachments and close relationships: A life-span perspective. In J.L. Gewirtz & W.M. Kurtines (Eds.), *Interaction with Attachment*. Hillsdale, NJ: Erlbaum.

Lewandowski, G., Aron, A., Bassis, S. & Kunak, J. (2006) Losing a self-expanding relationship: Implications for the self-concept. *Personal Relationships*, *13*(3), 317–331.

Lewandowski, G. & Bizzoco, N. (2007) Addition through subtraction: Growth following the dissolution of a low quality relationship. *The Journal of Positive Psychology*, *2*(1), 40–54.

Li, N.P. & Kenrick, D.T. (2006) Sex similarities and differences in preferences for short term mates: What, whether and why. *Journal of Personality and Social Psychology*, *90*, 468–489.

Lieberman, D. & Hatfield, E. (2006) Passionate love: Cross-cultural and evolutionary perspectives. In R.J. Sternberg & K. Weis (Ed.), *The Psychology of Love* (2nd edn). Cambridge, MA: Yale University Press.

Liebowitz, M.R. (1983) *The Chemistry of Love*. Boston, MA: Little, Brown & Co.

Lin, Y.-C. (1992) The construction of the sense of intimacy from everyday social interaction. Unpublished doctoral dissertation, University of Rochester, NY.

Lippert, T. & Prager, K.J. (2001) Daily experiences of intimacy: A study of couples. *Personal Relationships*, *8*, 283–298.

Livingstone, S. & Bober, M. (2005) *UK Children Go Online: Final Report of Key Project Findings*. London, UK: London School of Economics and Political Science.

Ljungberg, T., Horowitz, L., Jannson, J., Westlund, K. & Clarke, C. (2005) Communicative factors, conflict progression, and use of reconciliatory strategies in pre-school boys: A series of random events or a sequential process? *Aggressive Behavior*, *31*, 303–323.

Lloyd, S.A., Cate, R.M. & Henton, J.M. (1984) Predicting premarital relationship stability: A methodological refinement, *Journal of Marriage and the Family*, *46*, 71–76.

Locke, K.D. & Horowitz, L.M. (1990) Satisfaction in interpersonal interactions as a function of similarity in level of dysphoria. *Journal of Personality and Social Psychology*, *58*, 823–831.

Lundberg, J.K. & Sheehan, E.P. (1994) The effects of glasses and weight on perceptions of attractiveness and intelligence. *Journal of Social Behavior and Personality*, *9*, 753–760.

Maccoby, E.E. (1990) Gender and relationships: A developmental account. *American Psychologist*, *45*, 513–520.

Main, M. & Solomon, J. (1986) Discovery of a disorganized disorientated attachment pattern. In T.B. Brazelton & M.W. Yogman (Eds), *Affective Development in Infancy*. Norwood, NJ: Ablex.

Maner, J.K., DeWall, C.N. & Gailliot, M.T. (2008) Selective attention to signs of success: Social dominance and early stage interpersonal perception. *Personality and Social Psychology Bulletin*, *34*, 488–501.

Maner, J.K., Kenrick, D.T., Becker, D.V., Delton, A. W., Hofer, B., Wilbur, C. & Neuberg, S. (2003) Sexually selective cognition: Beauty captures the mind of the beholder. *Journal of Personality and Social Psychology*, *85*, 1107–1120.

Markey, P.M. & Markey, C.N. (2007) Romantic ideals, romantic obtainment and relationship experiences: The complementarity of interpersonal traits among romantic partners. *Journal of Social and Personal Relationships*, *24*, 517–534.

Markey, P.M. & Markey, C.N. (2009) Complementarity. In H. Reis & S. Sprecher (Eds), *Encyclopedia of Human Relationships*. Thousand Oaks, CA: Sage Publications.

Markey, P.M. & Markey, C.N. (2011) The complementarity of behavioral styles among lesbian couples. Paper presented at the annual meeting of the Society of Interpersonal Theory and Research, Zurich, Switzerland.

Marlowe, F. & Wetsman, A (2001) Preferred hip-to-ratio and ecology. *Personality and Individual Differences*, *30*, 481–489.

Massar, K. & Buunk, A.P. (2010) Judging a book by its cover: Jealousy after subliminal priming with attractive and unattractive faces. *Personality and Individual Differences*, *49*, 634–638.

McKillip, J. & Riedel, S.L. (1983) External validity of matching on physical attractiveness for same and opposite sex couples. *Journal of Applied Social Psychology*, *13*, 328–337.

McWhirter, D.P. & Mattison, A.M. (1984) *The Male Couple*. Englewood Cliffs, NJ: Prentice-Hall.

Mead, M. (1962) A cultural anthropologists's approach to maternal deprivation. In *World Health Organization, Deprivation of Maternal Care: A Reas-*

sessment of Its Effects (Public Health Papers, No. 14, pp. 45–62). Geneva, Switzerland: World Health Organization

Mehrabian, A. (1969) Some referents and measures of nonverbal behavior. *Behavioral Research Methods and Instruments*, 1, 213–217.

Messman, S.J., Canary, D.J. & Hause, K.S. (2000) Motives to remain platonic, equity, and the use of maintenance strategies in opposite-sex friendships. *Journal of Social & Personal Relationships*, 17, 67–94.

Miell, D. & Crogham, R. (1996) Examining the wider context of social relationships. In D. Miell & R. Dallos (Eds), *Social Interaction and Personal Relationships* (pp. 267–318). Milton Keynes, UK: Open University Press.

Mills, J., Clark, M.S., Ford, T.E. & Johnson, M. (2004) Measurement of communal strength. *Personal Relationships*, 11(2), 213–230.

Mok, D. & Wellman, B. (2007) Did distance matter before the Internet?: Interpersonal contact and support in the 1970s. *Social Networks*, 29(3), 430–461.

Mok, D., Carrasco, J.A. & Wellman, B. (2008) Does distance matter in the age of the internet? Paper presented at the International Sunbelt Social Network Conference, St. Petersburg, Florida.

Møller, A.P. & Alatalo, R.V. (1999) Good genes effects in sexual selection. *Proceedings of the Royal Society of London B*, 266, 85–91.

Mondloch, C.J., Lewis, T.L., Budreau, D.R., Maurer, D., Dannemiller, J.L., Stephens, B.R. & Kleinner-Gathercoal, K.A. (1999) Face perception during early infancy. *Psychological Science*, 10, 419–422.

Monroe, S., Rohde, P., Seeley, J. & Lewinsohn, P. (1999) Life events and depression in adolescence: Relationship loss as a prospective risk factor for first onset of major depressive disorder. *Journal of Abnormal Psychology*, 108(4), 606–614.

Moore, F.R. & Cassidy, C. (2007) Female status predicts female mate preferences across nonindustrial societies. *Cross-Cultural Research*, 41(1), 66–74.

Morton, J. & Johnson, M.H. (1991) CONSPEC and CONLERN: A two-way theory of infant face recognition. *Psychological Review*, 98, 164–181.

Murdock, G.P. (1949) *Social Structure*. New York Free Press.

Murdock, G.P. (1967) *Ethnographic Atlas*. Pittsburgh, PA: University of Pittsburg Press

Murstein, B.I. (1970) Stimulus–value–role: A theory of marital choice. *Journal of Marriage and the Family*, 32, 465–481.

Murstein, B.I. (1974) *Love, Sex and Marriage Through the Ages*. New York: Springer.

Murstein, B.I. (1976) *Who Will Marry Whom? Theories and Research in Marital Choice*. New York: Springer-Verlag.

Murstein, B.I. (1987) A clarification and extension of the SVR theory of dyadic parting. *Journal of Marriage and the Family*, 49, 929–933.

National Marriage Project. (1999) Social indicators of marital health and well-being: Trends in the past five decades.

Nehamow, L. & Lawton, M.P. (1975) Similarity and propinquity in friendship formation. *Journal of Personality and Social Psychology*, 32, 205–213.

Nix, C. (1999, November). But a 'real' friend wouldn't treat me that way! An examination of negative strategies employed in maintaining friendship. Paper presented at the National Communication Association Convention, Chicago, IL

Norton, M.L., Frost, J.H. & Ariely, D. (2007) Less is more: The lure of ambiguity, or why familiarity breeds contempt. *Journal of Personality and Social Psychology, 92*, 97–105.

Nuckolls, K.B., Cassell, J. & Kaplin, B.H. (1972) Psychosocial assets, life crisis and the prognosis of pregnancy, *American Journal of Epidemiology, 95*, 431–441.

Office of National Statistics. (2012) *Marriages in England and Wales 2010* (Release date 29 February 2012) Newport, UK: Office of National Statistics.

O'Leary, K.D. & Smith, D.A. (1991) Marital interaction, *Annual Review of Psychology, 42*, 191–212.

Oster, H., Daily, L. & Goldenthal, P. (1989) Processing facial affect. In A.W. Young & H.D. Ellis (Eds), *Handbook of Research on Face Processing* (pp. 107–161). Amsterdam: Elsevier.

Pataki, S.P., Shapiro, C. & Clark, M.S. (1994) Children's acquisition of appropriate norms for friendship and acquaintances. *Journal of Social and Personal Relations, 11*, 427–442.

Parke, R.D. (2004) Development in the family. *Annual Review of Psychology, 55*, 365–400.

Parke, R.D., Morris, K.L., Schofield, T.J., Leidy, M.S. & Flyr, M. (2006) Parent-child relationships: Contemporary perspectives. In P. Noller & J.A. Feeney (Eds), *Close Relationships: Functions, Forms and Processes*. Hove, UK: Psychology Press

Pascalis, O., de Haan, M. & Nelson, C.A. (2002) Is face processing species-specific during the first year of life? *Science, 296*, 1321–1323.

Pennington, D. (1986) *Essential Social Psychology*. London: Edward Arnold.

Peplau, L.A. & Cochran, S.D. (1980) Sex differences in values concerning love relationships. Paper presented at the Annual Meeting of the American Psycholological Association, September, Montreal, Canada.

Peplau, L.A., Cochran, S., Rook, K. & Padesky, C. (1978) Loving women: Attachment and autonomy in lesbian relationships. *Journal of Social Issues, 34*, 7–27.

Peplau, L. & Fingerhut, A. (2007) The close relationships of lesbians and gay men. *Annual Review of Psychology, 58*, 405–424.

Peplau, L. & Fingerhut, A. & Beals., K.P. (2004) Sexuality in the relationships of lesbians and gay men. In J.H. Harvey, A. Wenzel & S. Sprecher (Eds), *The Handbook of Sexuality in Close Relationships* (pp. 349–369). Mahwah. NJ: Lawrence Erlbaum Associates Inc.

Perlman, D. & Fehr, B. (1987) The development of intimate relationships. In D. Perlman & S. Duck (Eds), *Intimate Relationships: Development, Dynamics and Deterioration* (pp. 13–42). Beverly Hills, CA: Sage.

Perlman, D. (2007) The best of times, the worst of times: The place of close relationships in psychology and our daily lives. *Canadian Psychology, 48*(1), 7–18.

Peterson, D.R. (1983) Conflict. In H.H. Kelley (Ed.), *Close Relationships*. New York: Freeman.

Pillemer, J., Hatfield, E. & Sprecher, S. (2008) The importance of fairness and equity for the marital satisfaction of older women. *Journal of Women and Aging*, *20*, 215–230.

Plomin, R. (1994) Genetic Research and identification of environmental influences. *Journal of Child Psychology and Psychiatry*, *35*, 817–834.

Ponzetti, J. & James, C. (1997) Loneliness and sibling relationships. *Journal of Social Behavior and Personality*, *12*, 103–112.

Priest, J., Burnett, M., Thompson, R., Vogel, A. & Schvaneveldt, P. (2009) Relationship dissolution and romance and mate selection myths. *Family Science Review*, *14*, 48–57.

Prins, K.S., Buunk, A.P. & Van Yperen, N.W. (1992) Equity, normative disapproval and extramarital sex. *Journal of Social and Personal Relationships*, *10*, 39–53.

Ragsdale, J.D. & Brandau-Brown, F.E. (2005) Individual differences in the use of relational maintenance strategies in marriage. *Journal of Family Communication*, *5*, 61–75.

Rawlins, W.K. (1992) *Friendship Matters*. Hawthorne, NY: Aldine de Gruyter.

Regan, P. (2011) *Close Relationships*. New York: Routledge.

Reis, H.T. & Patrick, B.C. (1996) Attachment & Intimacy: Component processes. In E.T. Higgins & A.W. Kruglanski (Eds), *Social Psychology: Handbook of Basic Principles* (pp. 523–563). New York: Guildford Press.

Reis, H.T., Senchak, M. & Solomon, B. (1985) Sex differences in the intimacy of social interaction: Further examination of potential explanations. *Journal of Personality and Social Psychology*, *48*, 1204–1217.

Reis, H.T. & Shaver, P. (1988) Intimacy as an interpersonal process. In S. Duck (Ed.), *Handbook of Personal Relationships* (pp. 367–389). Chichester, UK: Wiley.

Rhodes, G. (2006) The evolutionary psychology of facial beauty. *Annual Review of Psychology*, *57*, 199–236.

Robles, T.F. & Kiecolt-Glaser, J.K. (2003) The physiology of marriage: Pathways to health. *Physiology and Behavior*, *79*, 409–416.

Rofé, Y. (1984) Stress and affiliation: A utility theory. *Psychological Review*, *91*(2), 235–250.

Rollie, S.S. & Duck, S. (2006) Stage theories and marital breakdown. In J.H. Harvey & M.A. Fine (Eds). *Handbook of Divorce and Dissolution of Romantic Relationships* (pp. 176–193). Mahwah, NJ: Lawrence Erlbaum Associates.

Rollins, B.C. & Feldman, H. (1970) Marital satisfaction over the family life cycle. *Journal of Marriage and the Family*, *32*, 20–28.

Rosenbaum, M.E. (1986) The repulsion hypothesis: on the nondevelopment of relationships. *Journal of Personality and Social Psychology*, *50*, 729–736.

Rubenstein, A.J., Kalkanis, L. & Langlois, J.H. (1999) Preferences for attractive faces: A cognitive explanation. *Developmental Psychology*, *35*, 848–855.

Rubin, Z. (1970) Measurement of romantic love. *Journal of Personality and Social Psychology*, *16*, 265–273.

Rubin, Z. (1973) *Liking and Loving*. New York: Holt, Rinehart and Winston.

Rusbult, C.E. (1983) A longitudinal test of the investment model. The development (and deterioration) of satisfaction and commitment in heterosexual involvement. *Journal of Personality and Social Psychology*, *45*, 101–117.

Rusbult, C.E. & Martz, J.M. (1995) Remaining in an abusive relationship: An investment model of nonvoluntary dependence. *Personality and Social Psychology Bulletin*, *21*, 558–571.

Rusbult, C.E. & Zembrodt, I.M. (1983) Responses to dissatisfaction in romantic involvements: A multidimensional scaling analysis. *Journal of Experimental Psychology*, *19*(3), 274–293.

Rusbult, C.E., Zembrodt, I.M. & Gunn, L.K. (1982) Exit, voice, and neglect: Responses to dissatisfaction in romantic involvements. *Journal of Personality and Social Psychology*, *43*, 1230–1242.

Rusbult, C.E., Farrell, D., Rogers, G. & Mainous, A.G. (1988) Impact of exchange variables on exit, voice, loyalty, and neglect: An integrative model of responses to declining job satisfaction. *Academy of Management Journal*, *31*, 599–627.

Sabourin, S., Lussier, Y. & Wright, J. (1991) The effects of measurement strategy on attributions for marital problems and behaviors. *Journal of Applied Social Psychology*, *21*, 734–746.

Sameroff, A.J. (1994) Developmental systems and family functioning. In R.D. Parke & S.G. Kellam (Eds), *Exploring family relationships with other social contexts* (pp. 199–214) Hillsdale, NJ: Lawrence Erlbaum Associates, Inc.

Sapadin, L.A. (1988) Friendship and gender: Perspectives of professional men and women. *Journal of Social & Personal Relationships*, *5*(4), 387–403

Sardar, Z. (1999) Why I didn't choose my wife. *New Statesman*.1 May, pp. 16–17.

Sardar, Z. (2008) First Person. *The Guardian*. 13 September 2008. Available from http://www.guardian.co.uk/lifeandstyle/2008/sep/13/family1 (Accessed 27 May, 2013)

Schachter, S. (1959) *The Psychology of Affiliation: Experimental Studies of the Sources of Gregariousness*. Stanford, CA: Stanford University Press.

Schaffer, H.R. (1996) *Social Development*. Oxford, UK: Blackwell.

Schaffer, H.R. & Emerson, P.E. (1964) The development of social attachments in infancy. *Monographs of the Society for Research on Child Development*. (Whole no. 29).

Schulz, R. & Sherwood, P.R. (2008) Physical and mental health effects of family caregiving. *American Journal of Nursing*, *108*, 23–27.

Sedikides, C., Oliver M.B. & Campbell, W.K. (1994) Perceived benefits and costs of romantic relationships for women and men: Implications for exchange theory. *Personal Relationships*, *1*, 5–21.

Segal, M.W. (1974) Alphabet and attraction: An unobstrusive measure of the effect of propinquity in a field setting. *Journal of Personality and Social Psychology*, *30*, 654–657.

Senchak, M. & Leonard, K.E. (1993) The role of spouses' depression and anger in the attribution marital satisfaction relation. *Cognitive Therapy and Research*, *17*(4), 397–412.

Shaffer, D.E., Smith, J.E. & Tomarelli, M. (1982) Self-monitoring as a determonat of self-disclosure reciprocity during the acquaintance process. *Journal of Personality & Social Psychology, 43*(1), 163–175.

Shaver, P., Hazan, C. & Bradshaw, D. (1988) Love as attachment: The integration of three behavioural systems. In R.J. Sternberg & M.L. Barnes (Eds.), *The Psychology of Love* (pp. 68–99). New Haven, CT: Yale University Press.

Sherif, M., Harvey, O.J., White, B.J., Hood, W.E. & Sherif, C.W. (1961) *Intergroup Conflict and Cooperation: The Robber's Cave Experiment.* Norman, OK: University of Oklahoma Press.

Sherrod, D. (1989) The influence of gender on same-sex friendships. In C. Hendrick (Ed.), *Review of Personality and Social Psychology: Vol. 10. Close Relationships* (pp. 164–186). Newbury Park, CA: Sage.

Shipman, B. & Smart, C (2007) 'It's made a huge difference': Recognition, rights and the personal significance of civil partnership. *Sociological Research Online, 12*(1), 1340.

Sigall, H. & Aronson, E. (1969) Liking for an evaluation as a function of her physical attractiveness and nature of the evaluation. *Journal of Experimental Social Psychology, 5*, 93–100.

Silverman, I. (1971) Physical attractiveness, *Sexual Behaviour*, September, 22–25.

Simon, R.B. (2002) Revisiting the relationships among gender, marital status, and mental health. *American Journal of Sociology, 107*(4), 1065–1096.

Simpson, J., Campbell, B. & Berscheid, E. (1986) The association between romantic love and marriage: Kephart (1967) twice revisited. *Personality and Social Psychology Bulletin, 12*, 363–372.

Simpson, J.A. (1990) Influence of attachment styles on romantic relationships. *Journal of Personality and Social Psychology, 59*, 971–980.

Singh, D. (1993) Adaptive significance of female attractiveness: Role of waist-to-hip ratio, *Journal of Personality and Social Psychology, 65*, 293–307.

Singh, D. & Luis, S. (1995) Ethnic and gender consensus for the effect of waist-to-hip ratio on judgement of women's attractiveness. *Human Nature, 6*, 51–65.

Smeaton, G., Byrne, D. & Murnen, S.K. (1989) The repulsion hypothesis revisited: Similarity irrelevance or dissimilarity bias? *Journal of Personality and Social Psychology, 56*, 54–59.

Smith, K.L., Tovée, M.J., Hancock, P., Bateson, M., Cox, M.A.A. & Cornelissen, P.L. (2007a). An analysis of body shape attractiveness based on image statistics: Evidence for a dissociation between expressions of preference and shape discrimination. *Visual Cognition, 15*, 1–27.

Smith, K.L., Cornelissen, P.L. & Tovée, M.J. (2007b). Color 3D bodies and judgements of human female attractiveness. *Evolution and Human Behavior, 28*, 48–54.

Sperling, M.B. & Borgaro, S. (1995) Attachment anxiety and reciprocity as moderators of interpersonal attraction. *Psychological Reports, 76*, 323–335.

Stafford, L. & Canary, D.J. (1991) Maintenance strategies and romantic relationship type, gender, and relational characteristics. *Journal of Social & Personal Relationships, 8*, 217–242.

Stafford, L., Dainton, M. & Haas, S. (2000) Measuring routine and strategic relational maintenance: scale revision, sex versus gender roles, and the prediction of relational characteristics. *Communication Monographs*, *67*, 306–323.

Stephen, T. (1985) Taking communication seriously: A reply to Murstein. *Journal of Marriage and the Family*, *47*, 937–938.

Sternberg, R.J. (1986) A triangular theory of love. *Psychological Review*, *93*(2), 119–135.

Sternberg, R.J. (1997) Construct validation of a triangular love scale. *European Journal of Social Psychology*, *27*, 313–335.

Stinson, D.A., Cameron, J.J., Wood, J.V., Gaucher, D. & Holmes, J.G. (2009) Deconstructing the 'reign of error': Interpersonal warmth explains the self-fulfilling prophecy of anticipated acceptance. *Personality and Social Psychology Bulletin*, *35*, 1165–1178.

Story, L.B., Karney, B.R., Lawrence, E. & Bradbury, T.N. (2004) Interpersonal mediators in the intergenerational transmission of marital dysfunction. *Journal of Family Psychology*, *18*(3), 519–529.

Straus, M.A. (1979) Measuring intrafamily conflict and violence: The Conflict Tactics Scales. *Journal of Marriage* and *the Family*, *41*, 75–88.

Straus, M.A. (1990) The Conflict Tactics Scale and its critics: An evaluation and new data on validity and reliability. In M.A. Straus & R.J. Gelles, *Physical Violence in American Families: Risk Factors and Adaptations to Violence in 8,145 Families* (pp. 49–73). New Brunswick, NJ: Transaction Publishing.

Straus, M.A., Gelles, R.J. & Steinmetz, S. (1980) *Behind Closed Doors: Violence in the American Family*. Garden City: NY: Anchor Books.

Streeter, S.A. & McBurney, D. (2003) Waist–hip ratio and attractiveness: New evidence and a critique for a critical test. *Evolution and Human Behavior*, *24*, 88–98.

Suls, J. & Wheeler, L. (2000) A selective history of classic social comparison theory and neo-social comparison theory. In J. Suls & L. Wheeler (Eds), *Handbook of Social Comparison: Theory and Research* (pp. 3–22). New York: Kluwer Academic/Plenum.

Surra, C.A. & Huston, T.L. (1987) Mate selection as a social transition. In D. Perlman & S. Duck (Eds.), *Intimate Relationships: Development, Dynamics and Deterioration* (pp. 88–120). Newbury Park, CA: Sage.

Swami, V. & Tovée, M.J. (2012) The impact of psychological stress on men's judgements of female body size. *PLoS ONE 7*(8): e42593. doi:10.1371/journal.pone.0042593

Tajfel, H. (1970) Experiments in intergroup discrimination. *Scientific American*, *223*, 96–102

Tatchell, P. (2005) Civil partnerships are divorced from reality. *The Guardian*, 19 December 2005.

Taylor, L.S., Fiore, A.T., Mendelsohn, G.A. & Cheshire, C. (2011) 'Out of my league': A real-world test of the matching hypothesis *Personality & Social Psychology Bulletin*, *37*(7), 942–954.

Thibaut, J.W. & Kelley, H.H. (1959) *The Social Psychology of Groups*. New York: Wiley.

Tolstedt, B.E. & Stokes, J.P. (1984) Self-disclosure, intimacy, and the depenetration process. *Journal of Personality and Social Psychology*, *46*, 84–90.

Tovée, M.J., Benson, P.J., Emery, J.L., Mason, S.M. & Cohen-Tovée, E.M. (2003) Measurement of body size and shape perception in eating disordered and control observers using body-shape software. *British Journal of Psychology*, *94*, 501–516.

Traupmann, J., Hatfield, E. & Wexler, P. (1983) Equity and sexual satisfaction in dating couples. *British Journal of Social Psychology*, *22*, 33–40.

Trivers, R.L. (1972) Parental investment and sexual selection. In B. Campbell (Ed.), *Sexual Selection and the Descent of Man* (pp. 136–179). Chicago: Aldine-Atherton.

Uchino, B.N. (2004) *Social Support and Physical Health: Understanding the Health Consequences of Relationships*. New Haven, CT: Yale University Press.

Unger, R. & Crawford, M. (1992) *Women and Gender: A Feminist Psychology*. New York: McGraw-Hill.

US Census Bureau. (2012) Table 133: Marriages and divorces—number and rate by state: 1990–2010. *The 2012 statistical abstract: The national data book* [online]. Retrieved from http://www.census.gov/compendia/statab/cats/births_deaths_marriages_divorces/marriages_and_divorces.html

Ustinov, P. (1979) *Dear Me*. New York: Penguin.

Van Ijzendoorn, M.H. & Sagi, A. (1999) Cross-cultural patterns of attachment: Universal and contextual dimensions. In J. Cassidy & P.R. Shaver (Eds), *Handbook of Attachment: Theory, Research, and Clinical Applications*. New York: Guilford Press.

Van Ijzendoorn, M.H. & Sagi, A. (1999) Cross-cultural patterns of attachment: Universal and contextual dimensions. In J. Cassidy & P.R. Shaver (Eds) *Handbook of Attachment: Theory, Research and Clinical Applications* (pp. 713–734). New York: Guilford Press.

Van Yperen, N.W. & Buunk, B.P. (1990) A longitudinal study of equity and satisfaction in intimate relationships. *European Journal of Social Psychology*, *20*, 287–309.

Wade, T.J. & Pevalin, D.J. (2004) Marital transitions and mental health. *Journal of Health and Social Behavior*, *45*, 155–170.

Waite, L.J. & Gallagher, M. (2000) *The Case for Marriage: Why Married People Are Happier, Healthier and Better Off Financially*. New York: Doubleday.

Walen, H. & Lachman, M.E. (2000) Social support and strain from partner, family and friends: Costs and benefits for men and women. *Journal of Social and Personal Relationships*, *17*, 5–30.

Walster, E., Aronson, V., Abrahams, D. & Rottmann, L. (1966) Importance of physical attractiveness in dating behaviour, *Journal of Personality and Social Psychology*, *4*, 508–516.

Walster, E., Walster, G.W. & Berschied, E. (1978) *Equity: Theory and Research*. Boston, MA: Allyn & Bacon.

Warr, P. (1983) Work, jobs and employment, *Bulletin of the British Psychological Society*, *36*, 305–311.

Wellman, B. (2001) Physical place and cyber-place: The rise of networked individualism. *International Journal for Urban and Regional Research, 25,* 227–252.

Wetsman, A. & Marlowe, F. (1999) How universal are preferences for female waist-to-hip ratios Evidence from the Hadza of Tanzania? *Evolution and Human Behavior, 20,* 219–228.

Whiting, B.B. & Edwards, C.P. (1988) *Children of Different Worlds.* Cambridge, MA: Harvard University Press.

Wilkinson, S. & Kitzinger, C. (2006) In support of equal marriage: Why civil partnership is not enough. *The Psychology of Women Section Review, 8*(1), 54–57.

Williams, K.D., Cheung, C.K.T. & Choi, W. (2000) CyberOstracism: Effects of being ignored over the internet. *Journal of Personality and Social Psychology, 79,* 748–762

Wilson, W. & Henzlik, W. (1986) Reciprocity of liking following face-to-face encounters with attractive and unattractive others. *Psychological Reports, 59,* 599–609.

Wright, P.H. (1982). Men's friendships, women's friendships and the alleged inferiority of the latter. *Sex Roles, 8,* 1–20.

Wright, P.H. (1984) Self referent motivation and the intrinsic quality of friendship. *Journal of Social & Personal Relationships, 1,* 114–130

Yinin, Y., Goldenberg, J. & Neeman, R. (1977) On the relationship structure of residence and formation of friendship, *Psychological Reports, 40,* 761–762.

Zajonc, R.B. (1968) Attitudinal effects of mere exposure. *Journal of Personality and Social Psychology, 8,* 1–29.

Zajonc, R.B. (2001) Mere exposure: A gateway to the subliminal. *Current Directions in Psychological Science, 10*(6), 224–228.

Zeifman, D. & Hazan, C. (2000) A process model of adult attachment formation. In W. Ickes & S. Duck (Eds), *The Social Psychology of Personal Relationships* (pp. 37–54). New York: Wiley.

Name Index

Subject index

Entries in **bold** indicate the page on which a key term is defined.